Number Three:
The W. L. Moody, Jr., Natural History Series

Common Texas Grasses

Common
TEXAS GRASSES
An Illustrated Guide
FRANK W. GOULD

With Guide to the Current Names of the Grasses
Stephan L. Hatch

 TEXAS A&M UNIVERSITY PRESS
College Station

Library of Congress Cataloging in Publication Data

Gould, Frank W.
    Common Texas grasses.

    (W. L. Moody, Jr., natural history series; no. 3)
    Includes index.
    1. Grasses–Texas–Identification.   I. Title.
II. Series.
QK495.G74G723   584'.9'09764   78-6368
ISBN 0-89096-058-5 pbk.

Manufactured in the United States of America
THIRD PRINTING, 1998

Contents

Preface

My recent basic taxonomic treatment of Texas grasses (*The Grasses of Texas*, Texas A&M University Press, 1975) has provided a manual for the study of the 523 species of native and introduced or adventive grasses of the state. Since the publication of that book, however, the need for a less technical, less inclusive treatment of the familiar and important grasses of the state has become increasingly evident. It is with this need in mind that the present volume has been prepared.

Included here is information about 150 of the most common and familiar grasses in Texas. Each species is illustrated and given a botanical description, together with information concerning its importance and where and under what conditions it grows. Field identification is facilitated by simplified keys to the species and a key to the genera. Although the botanical descriptions and the keys are given, as far as accuracy will allow, in laymen's terms, a glossary of many terms commonly used by botanists is also provided.

I am indebted to A. H. Walker, G. O. Hoffman, B. J. Ragsdale, and J. D. Rodgers, Texas A&M University System extension range specialists, for valuable information concerning the uses of range grasses. Data concerning growth and management of native forage grasses has been freely borrowed from the fine publication *100 Native Forage Grasses in 11 Southern States*, by H. L. Leithead, L. L. Yarlett, and T. N. Shiftlet (USDA Soil Conservation Service Agriculture Handbook No. 389, 1971).

Most of the excellent line drawings were prepared by Valloo Kapadia and Lucretia Hamilton. I have used these drawings in part in four previous books: *Grasses of the Texas Coastal Bend* (with T. W. Box; College Station: Texas A&M University, 1965), *Grasses of Southwestern United States* (Tucson: University of Arizona Biological Science Bulletin No. 7, 1951), *Grass Systematics* (New York: McGraw-Hill Book Co., 1968), and *The Grasses of Texas*. Preparation of the illustrations by Valloo Kapadia was supported by a grant from the Rob and Bessie Welder Wildlife Foundation.

A few of the excellent illustrations from Hitchcock's *Manual of the Grasses of the United States* have been included here. They are of *Arundo donax, Erianthus giganteus, Festuca arundinacea* (as *F. elatior*), *Lolium perenne* (in part, as *L. multiflorum*), *Melica nitens, Paspalum urvillei*, and *Polypogon monspeliensis*. I am also indebted to the McGraw-Hill Book

Company for permission to use the following grass illustrations from *Grass Systematics: Arundinaria gigantea, Briza minor*, and *Scleropogon brevifolius*.

Permission has also been granted by the University of Arizona Press to use the following illustrations originally prepared by Lucretia Hamilton for *Grasses of Southwestern United States*: Figs. 3 and 5 showing the structure of the plant and flowers, florets, and spikelets; and twenty-three grass illustrations, namely, *Andropogon gerardii, Bouteloua aristidoides, B. barbata, B. eriopoda, B. gracilis, B. hirsuta, B. rigidiseta, Buchloë dactyloides, Cynodon dactylon, Digitaria californica* (as *Trichachne californica*), *Elymus canadensis, Eragrostis intermedia, Erioneuron pulchellum, Heteropogon contortus, Hilaria belangeri* (plant), *H. mutica, Koeleria pyramidalis* (as *K. cristata*), *Leptochloa dubia, Muhlenbergia porteri, Panicum obtusum, Sporobolus airoides, S. cryptandrus*, and *Stipa comata*.

All other illustrations, with the added exception of twenty-six new figures presented here for the first time, are from Grasses of the Texas Coastal Bend and The Grasses of Texas. The new figures, prepared by Lucretia Hamilton, are for the grass flower and three spikelet types, *Andropogon ternarius, Aristida roemeriana, A. wrightii, Avena fatua* (spikelet), *Bothriochloa barbinodis* var. *perforata* (spikelet), *Bouteloua rigidiseta, Brachiaria ciliatissima, Bromus tectorum, Cenchrus myosuroides* (inflorescence), *Cortaderia selloana, Dichanthelium acuminatum, D. laxiflorum, Digitaria ciliaris, Echinochloa crus-pavonis* var. *macera, Enneapogon desvauxii, Eragrostis curvula, E. trichodes, Erioneuron pilosum, Lolium temulentum, Melica nitens, Panicum amarum, P. coloratum, P. hemitomon, Phragmites australis, Tridens flavus*, and *Uniola paniculata*.

COMMON TEXAS GRASSES

Introduction

The importance of grasses to mankind often is not fully realized. Cereal grains such as rice, corn or maize, wheat, oats, and barley provide a large proportion of the plant food products consumed directly by humans. Meat and poultry, important to Texans' diets, are indirect products of grass forage and grass grain crops.

Grasses provide cover and food for the many types of large and small wild animals that inhabit our rangelands and together contribute to the composition and quality of our natural areas. Grasses provide the best means of checking soil erosion on rangelands. Roots, runners, and litter from the annual replacement of leafy stems are not only soil stabilizers but soil builders as well. In urban areas, the sod grasses or turf grasses provide the aesthetic benefits of lawns and parks as well as green fields for sports and recreation. Probably of equal value in the city is grass's ability to reduce dust in the atmosphere and dirt in the streets.

The Grass Plant

Grasses characteristically are tufted or sod-forming herbaceous plants with narrow, elongate leaves. The annual grass completes its entire life cycle in one year or less, but perennial grass stems (culms) die back to the persistent base and are replaced by new shoots each year. Only the bamboos have woody stems that function for more than one year. Several species of bamboo have been introduced into Texas, but only the shrubby giant cane or switch cane (*Arundinaria gigantea*) is native.

Grasses are flowering plants grouped in the monocotyledonous family Poaceae and distantly related to the sedge, lily, and rush families. The grass plant (Fig. I) consists of stems (culms), roots, leaves, and inflorescences of small flowers borne in specialized structures called *spikelets.* The spikelet, referred to as "the basic unit of grass classification," usually is the most readily recognizable structure of the grass plant, and the exact identity of a grass can often be determined on the basis of a single spikelet.

Stems. Grass stems are generally smooth and cylindrical. They are made up of elongated, hollow, solid, or semisolid sections called *internodes* that are connected by solid, often swollen *nodes.* Leaves, branches, and adventitious roots are produced at the nodes.

As the young grass embryo develops, it soon forms a leafy shoot with

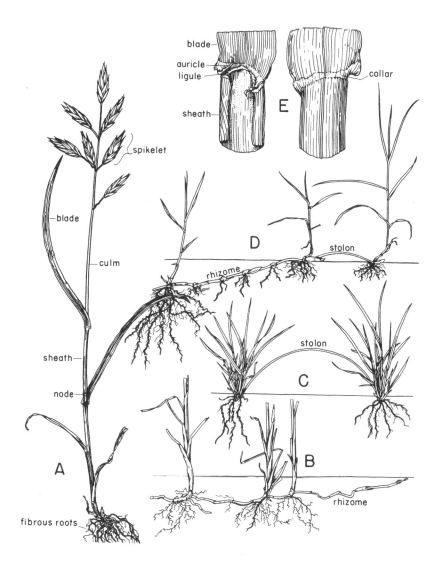

Fig. I. Structure of the grass plant: A, general habit *(Bromus unioloides)*; B, rhizomes; C, stolon; D, rhizome and stolon intergradation *(Cynodon dactylon)*; and E, the leaf at the junction of sheath and blade, showing adaxial surface (left) and abaxial surface (right).

4 : Common Texas Grasses

growing areas at the tip (the *apical meristem* or *growing point*) and just above each stem node (the *intercalary meristems*). The intercalary meristems make it possible for the stem to continue growing below the growing point at the tip of the shoot. As the stem tissue matures, the tender growing areas both at the nodes and at the shoot tip are protected by the sheathing leaf bases. Only after the lower part of the shoot is well established does the flowering shoot tip emerge from its protective cloak of leaves.

Botanists usually refer to erect grass stems as *culms*. Stems that run or loop along the surface of the ground and root at the nodes are termed *stolons*. Buffalograss (*Buchloë dactyloides*) and burrograss (*Scleropogon brevifolius*) form extensive colonies by the development of stolons. Stems that run under the surface of the soil are termed *rhizomes*. Western wheatgrass (*Agropyron smithii*) and seashore dropseed (*Sporobolus virginicus*) are important grasses that develop extensive rhizome systems. Some sod grasses such as Bermudagrass (*Cynodon dactylon*) have both rhizomes and stolons. Rhizomes may be distinguished from root structures by their nodes and internodes and often by the presence of scalelike leaves as well as roots at the nodes.

Roots. All grass roots are fibrous and generally similar in appearance. In the germinating seed and in the young seedling the roots are all part of the primary root system. Soon after the establishment of the seedling, however, *adventitious roots* are freely developed at the lower stem nodes, and after a few weeks they take over all of the root functions. Roots are important to the grass plant for the uptake of water and mineral nutrients, for the support of the leafy, flower-bearing shoots, and to a lesser extent for the storage of food materials.

Leaves. Grass leaves are borne in two ranks or rows alternately at successive nodes of the stem. The leaf consists of a flattened *blade* jointed to a *sheath* that surrounds the stem. The sheath usually is split to its base on one side, but in a few grasses, such as rescuegrass (*Bromus unioloides*), the margins of the sheath are united to near its apex. At the junction of sheath and blade there is usually a distinct zone of specialized cells; the outside of this area is termed the *collar*, and the inside is referred to as the *throat*.

The blades of most grasses are flat and *linear* (with parallel sides) or *lanceolate* (tapering to a point from or immediately above the base). In a few species, especially those of dry regions, the blades become inrolled (*involute*). Most grass blades have a prominent slender vein or rib, called the *midnerve*, and a few or several lateral ribs (*nerves*). The leaf margin commonly is smooth, roughened with short, stiff *spicules*, or bordered with a row of hairs (*ciliate*).

At the base of the blade on the inner surface there usually is a thin, membranous rim or ring of hairs called the *ligule*, the exact function of which is unknown. The *ligule* often looks like an extension of the sheath tip. Membranous lobes or projections of tissue termed *auricles* occasionally are present at the upper end of the sheath or at the base of the blade. Indiangrass (*Sorghastrum nutans*), for example, usually has stiff, pointed auricles on either side of the apex of the sheath, while cultivated oats (*Hordeum vulgare*) has thin, membranous leaf auricles.

The Inflorescence. The flowering tip of the grass shoot is termed the *inflorescence*. The arrangement of spikelets in the flower cluster or inflorescence is of great importance in grass classification. The inflorescence is limited at its base by the uppermost stem node. The spikelets may be stalked (*pediceled*) or stalkless (*sessile*) on the main axis (*rachis*) of the inflorescence or on branches. Three general types of grass inflorescence are recognized: spikes, racemes, and panicles.

The *spike* is an inflorescence with all the spikelets stalkless on the main stem, or axis, as in wheat (*Triticum aestivum*) and perennial ryegrass (*Lolium perenne*).

The *raceme* is an inflorescence with the spikelets either stalked or both stalkess and stalked on an unbranched axis. Little barley (*Hordeum pusillum*) and little bluestem (*Schizachyrium*) are examples.

Most grass inflorescences are *panicles*, with the spikelets stalkless or stalked on branches. The branches may be spreading or tightly compressed. Plains lovegrass (*Eragrostis intermedia*) and Hall panicum (*Panicum hallii*) have open panicles with two or more degrees of branching. Many grasses have specialized panicles in which the spikelets are stalkless or short-stalked on the primary branches, as in sideoats grama (*Bouteloua curtipendula*) and Bermudagrass (*Cynodon dactylon*).

In grasses of the *Andropogon* tribe (Andropogoneae) the spikelets occur in pairs of one stalkless and one stalked. In Johnsongrass (*Sorghum halepense*) and other andropogonoid grasses with freely branched panicles, the spikelets are in threes, one stalkless and two stalked, at the branch tips.

Flowers and Spikelets. All grasses have flowers, but the flowers are small and inconspicuous and hidden in the protective scales (*bracts*) of the *spikelets* (Fig. II). The spikelet itself is a greatly reduced and modified flowering branch, with one or several flowers on a short central axis called the *rachilla*. Each flower with its protective scales is termed a *floret*. The grass flower usually consists of a single-celled ovary, or *pistil*, three male *stamens*, and two thin or fleshy mounds called *lodicules*.

At the base of the spikelet there are usually two bracts, the *glumes*, that do not contain flowers. Above the glumes, one or more *florets* are developed alternately at the nodes of the rachilla. Each floret usually consists of two bracts called the *lemma* and the *palea*, which enclose a flower between them. Usually the only evidence of the flower in the floret is the feathery stigmas of the ovary and the anthers of the stamens, which

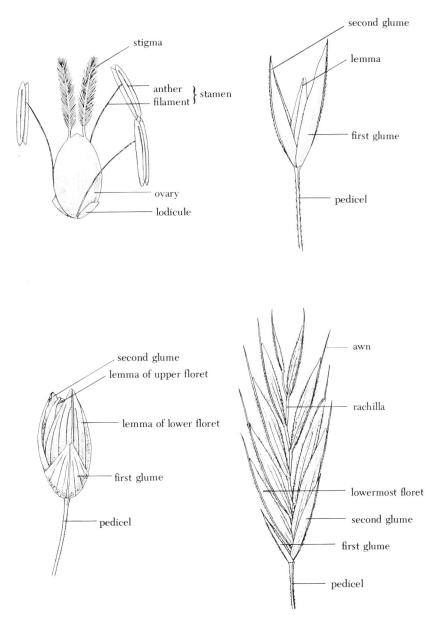

Fig. II.   Structure of the grass flower and spikelet types: *A*, the grass flower; *B*, *Agrostis* spikelet with one floret; *C*, *Panicum* spikelet with two florets; and *D*, *Bromus* spikelet with nine florets.

often project out of the bracts at flowering time. In time, the fruit or grain becomes visible in some types of grass.

In a few grasses, such as southern wildrice (*Zizaniopsis miliacea*), male flowers, with stamens only, and female flowers, with a pistil only, are borne in separate spikelets on the same plant (*monoecious*). In other species, such as buffalograss (*Buchloë dactyloides*), male and female spikelets are borne on separate plants (*dioecious*). In buffalograss the male and female spikelets are strikingly different, and plants of the two sexes can easily be mistaken for different species.

In grass identification it is important to note the number of florets in each spikelet and the character of the glumes and lemmas. Often the midnerve of the glume or lemma is extended into a bristle or *awn*, and occasionally the lemma is many-awned, as in feather pappusgrass (*Enneapogon desvauxii*), a small, tufted perennial of the arid Southwest. In the familiar threeawn grasses of the genus *Aristida*, the lemma of the single floret is elongated and tipped by three awns which are fused together at their base to form a short or long *awn column*.

In *Panicum* and related grasses the spikelets regularly have two florets, with the upper floret well developed and seed-bearing (*perfect*) and the lower floret neuter or male (*staminate*, with stamens only). In big bluestem (*Andropogon gerardii*) and other grasses of the *Andropogon* tribe, the spikelets are in pairs of one stalked and one stalkless and the outer bract of the spikelet, the first glume, is thicker and firmer than the rest of the spikelet, which it enfolds or partially encloses.

Fruits. The mature grain of the grass commonly is referred to as grass seed. Actually, the "grain" may be the ripened ovary (botanically a fruit), the ovary plus the two bracts of the floret (lemma and palea), the entire spikelet, or, as in the "seed" of buffalograss, a cluster of spikelets.

Technically, most grass fruits are *caryopses*, which are defined as dry, one-seeded fruits which remain closed at maturity (*indehiscent*), with the ovary wall stuck to the seed coat. The grass seed is always enclosed in the small, dry ovary, but in the dropseeds (*Sporobolus*) and a few other grasses the seed is free from the ovary wall and can be expelled from the ovary wall when the grain is moistened.

Identifying Grasses

To anyone familiar with grasses, the many species present in Texas are often recognizable at a glance. Recognition frequently is based on gross characters such as leaf size, color, and "feel," the longevity of the plant, the type of clump or sod it forms, the time of the year it "greens up," the general appearance of the inflorescence and the seed units, and the association of the grass in question with other grasses and forbes. To anyone not familiar with grasses, however, reliable identification of an unknown grass is by necessity based on technical characters of the inflorescence and the spikelet. These characters tend to be much more consistent than features of the stems and leaves, which vary considerably with age and differences in growing conditions.

Many people who would like to be able to identify grasses are intimidated by the seeming complexity of the spikelet parts, their smallness, and the unfamiliar terms used to refer to them. With some experience, however, most people find that the grass flower parts are really much simpler than they first seem. A hand magnifying lens with a magnification of 8× or 10× is essential for examining the tiny spikelet parts, and dissecting needles, which can be made by imbedding the eyes of heavy sewing needles in the ends of wooden dowel handles, and tweezers are also useful in separating the parts for study.

A collection or file of dried grass plants will allow repeated reference to the grasses that grow in a local area. To dry a grass specimen, fold it in several sheets of newspaper to about 12 × 16 inches and dry it under pressure, replacing the "blotter" newspaper each day until the specimen is completely dry. Then mount the specimen with spots of cement on a large sheet of stiff paper or cardboard and store it in a file folder. Enter the grass name along with the place and date of collection in a notebook. If the collection grows large enough, you may wish to number each specimen sheet and enter the number in the notebook along with the specimen record.

Measurements of grass structures in this book are given in units of the metric system. As can be seen on the comparative metric and inch scales, one centimeter (cm) is slightly less than one-half inch, and fifteen centimeters is about equal to six inches. In the measurement of tall grass stems, one meter (m) is about equal to one yard.

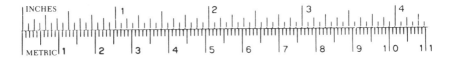

Fig. 1.   Western wheatgrass *(Agropyron smithii)* plant and spikelet.

10 : Common Texas Grasses

Accounts of the Grasses

AGROPYRON

1. Western wheatgrass (bluestem; bluejoint) *Agropyron smithii* Rydb.

Perennial with slender, firm stems mostly 30–90 cm tall from creeping rhizomes, the stems single or in small clusters. *Sheaths* hairless or the lower ones softly hairy, often with a short fringe along the upper margins and with or without slender, pointed auricles on either side of the collar. *Ligule* a minutely fringed membrane about 1 mm long. *Blades* firm, stiff, and hairless or somewhat hairy on the upper surface, 2–7 mm broad, tapering to a long, slender tip, and usually inrolled when dried. *Inflorescence* a spike 6–20 cm long, with the large, several-flowered spikelets closely placed and typically one per node but occasionally paired at the lower and middle nodes. At maturity the nodes come apart (disarticulate) above the glumes. *Internodes of inflorescence axis* flattened but thick, averaging about 7–10 mm long but sometimes much longer. *Spikelets* mostly 1.5–2.5 cm long and with five to twelve flowers. *Glumes* slightly unequal, firm, and narrowly lanceolate, with three to seven nerves, usually tapering from a broadened base to a narrowly pointed or short-awned tip, and the second glume usually equaling or exceeding the lowermost lemma. *Lemmas* firm, with several indistinct nerves and hairless or hairy margins. Plants setting seed mostly from May to July, occasionally in late summer and fall.

DISTRIBUTION AND HABITAT. Western wheatgrass is found in north-central and western Texas, usually in clay or clay-loam soils but also in sand. It is most frequent on low, moist flats or floodplains. It ranges throughout western North America from Canada to northern Texas, New Mexico, and Arizona.

USE. This grass is a native cool-season perennial that provides good grazing for livestock and fair grazing for antelope and other wildlife. In many areas of the West it is considered to be one of the most valuable native grasses, but in Texas western wheatgrass rarely contributes a significant amount of range forage.

Fig. 2. Winter bentgrass *(Agrostis hiemalis)* plant and spikelet.

12 : Common Texas Grasses

AGROSTIS

2. Winter bentgrass (winter redtop) *Agrostis hiemalis* (Walt.) B.S.P.

Tufted perennial with slender, usually stiffly erect stems 15–70 cm tall. *Stems and leaves* hairless. Leaves mostly from the base, the blades flat or inrolled, linear, 0.5–3 mm broad. *Ligule* a membrane mostly 1.5–4 cm long. *Panicles* loose and open, delicate, and much-branched at maturity, 7–30 cm or more long. *Panicle branches* slender and bent or wavy, at least some 5–15 cm or more long, branching at the middle or above and with spikelets only near the tips. *Spikelets* one-flowered, awnless, closely placed and overlapping, 1.5–2.1 mm long. *Glumes* pointed, the first glume often slightly longer than the second. *Lemmas* thin, translucent, and slightly shorter than the glumes. *Paleas* absent. Plants setting seed mostly March to May.

DISTRIBUTION AND HABITAT. Winter bentgrass is distributed almost throughout Texas in pastures, in open woods, along roadsides, and on ditch banks, usually in moist, sandy soil.

USE. This species is a cool-season weak perennial of only fair forage value for livestock and wildlife. It produces little herbage, and its main value is in the relatively abundant production of birdseed.

ALOPECURUS

3. Carolina foxtail *Alopecurus carolinianus* Walt.

Tufted annual with stems mostly 10–50 cm long. *Sheaths* usually much shorter than stem internodes. *Ligule* a membrane 3.5–7 mm long. *Blades* flat, weak, 3–15 cm long and 1–5 mm broad. *Panicles* short, cylindrical, 2–6 cm long, 4–6 mm thick. *Spikelets* one-flowered. *Glumes* equal, awnless, abruptly rounded at the tips, hairy on the thick midnerve and margins. *Lemmas* hairless, rounded at the tip, with the midnerve projecting as an awn 3–5 mm long from the base or near the base. *Anthers* minute, 0.3–0.5 mm long. *Grain* 1–1.4 mm long. Plants setting seed mostly March to June.

DISTRIBUTION AND HABITAT. Found throughout the eastern half of Texas, Carolina foxtail is frequent during the spring months, but it is usually inconspicuous in moist, often disturbed soils of pastures and along streams, ditches, borders of woods, and roadways.

USE. A grass of little economic significance, this species possibly supplies appreciable amounts of birdseed, as do the other annual, cool-season grasses with which it is associated.

Fig. 3. Carolina foxtail *(Alopecurus carolinianus)* inflorescence and spikelet.

ANDROPOGON

Key to the species:

Stalked spikelet large, well developed, usually with stamens but not pistils .... Big bluestem, A. *gerardii*

Stalked spikelet rudimentary, either much reduced or entirely absent and represented by the stalk only

Stalkless spikelet 5–7 mm long; central axis of inflorescence branches stiff and straight .... Splitbeard bluestem, A. *ternarius*

Stalkless spikelet 4 mm or less long; central axis of inflorescence branch slender and bent or wavy

Flowering stem profusely branched and rebranched, broomlike, with the branchlets and terminal sheaths greatly reduced and crowded; main stems tall and coarse ....
.... Bushy bluestem, A. *glomeratus*

Flowering stem moderately rebranched, not broomlike; main stem slender, moderately tall ....
.... Broomsedge bluestem, A. *virginicus*

4. Big bluestem (turkeyfoot) *Andropogon gerardii* Vitman

Tall, stout perennial either with or without rhizomes. *Stems* in small to large clumps, mostly 0.8–2 m tall. *Leaves* green or with a whitish waxy coating, usually hairless. *Blades* long, linear, flat, rather firm, mostly 5–10 mm broad. *Inflorescence* of two to seven spikelike branches, these typically 4–11 cm long. *Spikelets* in pairs of one stalkless and bisexual and one stalked and male (with stamens only). *Stalkless spikelets* 7–11 mm long, usually rough, often with a whitish waxy coating, and more or less "boat-shaped," with a double-keeled first glume and a single-keeled second glume of equal length. *Lemma* of stalkless spikelet thin, mostly membranous, deeply cleft, and with slender, bristle-tipped lobes at the tip on either side of a stout awn. *Lemma awn* hairless, bent and twisted at its base. *Stalked spikelet* usually about as large as the stalkless one, awnless. Plants flowering mostly August through November.

DISTRIBUTION AND HABITAT. This native, warm-season perennial is distributed nearly throughout the state. It usually is associated with other tall grasses in prairies and openings in woods and does best in rich, sandy soils. It has good leaf development in the spring and sets seed mostly in summer and early fall.

USE. Big bluestem provides good grazing for livestock during the growing period and makes good hay when cut at the time of seed production. In Texas it is rated as poor forage for deer, but it contributes significantly to wildlife habitat.

Fig. 4.   Big bluestem *(Andropogon gerardii)* plant, spikelet pair, and spikelet.

5. Bushy bluestem   *Andropogon glomeratus* (Walt.) B.S.P.

Perennial with stems stiffly erect, mostly 75–150 cm tall, in small clumps. *Sheaths* usually hairless, less frequently hairy along the margins and on the back near the collar, with the lower sheaths broad, overlapping, strongly compressed laterally, and keeled on the back. *Blades* elongate, frequently folded, mostly 2.5–6 mm broad, and usually much narrower than the sheaths. *Flowering stems* profusely branched and rebranched, the ultimate branches broomlike, with their reduced, long-

Fig. 5.   Bushy bluestem *(Andropogon glomeratus)* mass of inflorescences at the stem tip.

haired inflorescences. *Uppermost branchlets* covered with silky down, at least just below the nodes. *Sheaths of the terminal branchlets* much reduced, narrow, and typically colored reddish brown or bronze. *Inflorescence branches* usually paired, 1.5–3 cm long, slightly shorter than the sheath below and partially enclosed by it, delicate, not flattened or only slightly flattened, and hairy with long, soft, silvery hairs. *Stalkless*

Fig. 6. Splitbeard bluestem *(Andropogon ternarius)* plant.

spikelets one-seeded, usually 3–4.5 mm long, the glumes hairless. *Awn of lemma* straight to wavy, not sharply bent, 1–2 cm long. *Spikelet stalk* slender, cylindrical or slightly flattened, and densely covered with long hairs. *Stalked spikelets* rudimentary or completely absent. Plants flowering mostly September to November, but occasionally producing seed throughout the year.

DISTRIBUTION AND HABITAT. Reported from all regions of the state, bushy bluestem is usually present in low, moist sites in relatively sterile soils. It is frequently associated with broomsedge bluestem in weedy plant growth on range in poor condition. Usually the bushy bluestem plants will be in low, moist sites along ditches, tanks, and marshy areas, and the broomsedge bluestem plants will be in the slightly higher and drier soils immediately above.

USE. Bushy bluestem is a poor forage grass for livestock and wildlife, but it often provides good cover for wild animals and birds.

6. Splitbeard bluestem *Andropogon ternarius* Michx.

Tufted perennial with stems mostly 70–120 cm tall, the plants usually forming small clumps. *Stems* entirely hairless or with a tuft of long, silvery hairs just below the uppermost leaf-bearing or bract-bearing node. *Basal leaves* with broad, hairless, stiff-haired, or densely soft-haired sheaths and narrow blades frequently 20 cm or more long. *Blades* elongate, mostly 2–4 mm broad, and hairless or the lower ones sparsely stiff-haired. *Inflorescence* usually with two densely hairy, paired branches 3–6 cm long, these commonly well extended above the uppermost leaf or bract and less frequently partially enclosed in an enlarged sheath. Inflorescences often developed on lateral shoots at all upper stem nodes, the branches and spikelet stalks densely covered with soft, silvery hairs mostly 6–9 mm long. *Stalkless spikelets* 5–7 mm long excluding the lemma awn. *Glumes* hairless. *Lemma of upper floret* with a translucent membranous body and a slender, loosely twisted, and somewhat bent awn, 1.5–2.5 cm long, from a deeply forked apex. *Stalked spikelet* reduced to a slender, awnless rudiment usually 2 mm or less long. Plants producing seed mostly from September to November, but occasionally as early as June.

DISTRIBUTION AND HABITAT. In eastern and central Texas splitbeard bluestem is commonly found on sandy, well-drained soils in open pastures, borders of woods, and cut-over woodland pastures.

USE. This warm-season, perennial bunch grass provides good forage during the growing season for livestock and fair forage for deer and other wildlife. It often is associated with little bluestem and occasionally with silver bluestem. Although it sometimes forms large colonies, splitbeard bluestem seldom is sufficiently abundant to be a key management species.

7. Broomsedge bluestem *Andropogon virginicus* L.

Perennial with slender stems in small tufts or clumps. *Stems* stiffly erect, mostly 50–100 cm tall, branching above to produce several inflorescences, but not as profusely branched as bushy bluestem. *Stem nodes* hairless. *Stems and leaves* hairless, or sheaths and blades variously hairy, the hairs, when present, usually sparse and occurring only along the margins. *Sheaths* usually broader than the blades, laterally com-

Fig. 7. Broomsedge bluestem *(Andropogon virginicus)* stem tip with three inflorescences and spikelet with attached stalk of a vestigial spikelet.

pressed, and sharply keeled on the midnerve. *Blades* elongate, flat or folded, mostly 2–5 mm broad. *Inflorescences* several on each flowering stem, usually with two to five slender, bent or wavy, spikelike branches 2–3 cm long, partially enclosed in slightly enlarged, yellowish, straw-colored, or slightly bronze-tinged bracts. *Leafy bracts* of inflorescence mostly 3 6 cm long and 2–5 mm broad. *Nodes and upper portion of stem internode below terminal sheath* usually hairless or with a few long hairs, and occasionally with a tuft of hairs. *Spikelet axis and stalk* slender and covered with long, silky hairs. *Stalkless spikelets* mostly 2.5–4 mm long, the lemma with an awn 1–2 cm long. *Stalked spikelets* greatly reduced or absent. Plants producing seed mostly September through November.

DISTRIBUTION AND HABITAT. Found throughout the eastern third of the state, broomsedge bluestem occurs mostly on loose, sandy, moist soils, often in overgrazed pastures and old fields.

USE. A warm-season, native perennial of value for wildlife habitat but of little value for livestock or wildlife forage, broomsedge bluestem frequently grows intermingled with bushy bluestem, but for the most part it occupies higher and drier sites. In the field it can be readily distinguished from the bushy bluestem by its more slender appearance, shorter and less densely flowered stems, and lighter-colored (usually straw-colored) herbage and inflorescence bracts. In Texas the stem of broomsedge bluestem is hairless, or nearly so, below the spathelike inflorescence sheaths, whereas in bushy bluestem there is a tuft of long hairs below the sheath. Broomsedge bluestem is seldom grazed by any kind of animal, and it tends to invade overgrazed ranges in the eastern, coastal, and southern parts of the state.

ARISTIDA

Key to the species:
Lemma 16 mm or more long to the base of the awns; plants annual ...
.... Oldfield threeawn, A. *oligantha*
Lemma less than 16 mm long to the base of the awns, or if this long, then
  plants perennial
  Plants annual; awns 6–35 mm long
    Central awn 5–15 mm long and bent sharply backwards at least on
      some spikelets; lateral awns one-third to slightly over one-half
      as long as the central awn ....
      .... Slimspike threeawn, A. *longespica* var. *longespica*
    Central awn 15–35 cm long and typically not bent sharply backwards;
      lateral awns usually two-thirds to three-fourths as long as the
      central awn ....
      .... Kearney threeawn, A. *longespica* var. *geniculata*
  Plants perennial; awns 15–50 mm long
    Panicle open or loose, the main branches slender and short, and at
      least some curving in a U or S shape under the weight of the
      spikelets
      Lemmas 6–9 mm long to the base of the awns; awns 1.5–2.8 cm
        (occasionally up to 3.5 cm) long ....
        .... Roemer threeawn, A. *roemeriana*
      Lemmas usually 10–16 mm long to the base of the awns; awns
        mostly 3–10 cm long
        Awns 5–10 cm or more long; second glume usually 16–25 mm

long; lemmas mostly 13–16 mm long including the awn
column .... Red threeawn, *A. longiseta*
Awns 3–4.5 cm long; second glume usually 15 mm or less long;
lemmas mostly 10–12 mm long including the awn column .... Purple threeawn, *A. purpurea*
Panicle contracted, the branches usually all stiffly pressed closely
against the main branches ..... Wright threeawn, *A. wrightii*

8. *Aristida longespica* Poir.

Tufted annual with slender, wiry stems 20–60 cm tall, these freely
branched at the lower nodes. *Leaves* not in a conspicuous basal tuft.

Fig. 8a.   Slimspike threeawn (*Aristida longespica* var. *longespica*) inflorescence
and spikelet.

Fig. 8b.   Kearney threeawn *(Aristida longespica* var. *geniculata)* inflorescence and spikelet.

Sheaths hairless, or the lower ones hairy and often with a few long hairs in the vicinity of the ligule. *Blades* slender and threadlike, flat or inrolled, mostly 0.5–1 mm broad. *Inflorescence* a slender, contracted panicle with spikelets pressed closely against the main stalk and on short branches. *Glumes* usually about equal, abruptly pointed or tapering to a slender tip, the second occasionally slightly three-lobed. *Lemmas* slender, often mottled or barred with purple.

Key to the varieties:
Central awn mostly 5–15 mm long and bent sharply backwards on at least
    some spikelets; lateral awns one-third to slightly over one-half as long
    as the central awn . . . .
    . . . . Slimspike threeawn, A. *longespica* var. *longespica*

Central awn 15–36 mm (occasionally as little as 12 mm) long, typically not
    bent sharply backwards; lateral awns usually two-thirds to three-
    fourths as long as the central awn . . . .
    . . . . Kearney threeawn, A. *longespica* var. *geniculata*

8a. Slimspike threeawn *Aristida longespica* Poir. var. *longespica*
    Inflorescences mostly 10–20 cm long, usually with few and widely
spaced spikelets. *Lemmas* 4–8 mm long to base of awns, with the middle
awn mostly 6–15 cm long, bent sharply backwards, and with much shorter erect or sharply bent lateral awns. Plants setting seed late August to
November.
    DISTRIBUTION AND HABITAT. Slimspike threeawn is a grass of eastern
Texas and is most frequent in loose, sandy soils.
    USE. A rather common short-lived, warm-season, native annual, this
variety develops little herbage and provides essentially no forage for livestock or wildlife.

8b. Kearney threeawn *Aristida longespica* Poir. var. *geniculata* (Raf.)
    Fern.
    Inflorescence mostly 15–35 cm long. *Lemmas* 7–9 mm long to the
base of the awns. *Lemma awns* spreading, some infrequently bent sharply
backwards, with the central awn 15–36 mm long and the lateral awns
slightly shorter. For the most part, Kearney threeawn tends to be larger
and to have larger spikelets and longer awns than slimspike threeawn.
Plants setting seed late August to December.
    DISTRIBUTION AND HABITAT. Kearney threeawn is found in the eastern
two-thirds of the state, usually in sandy soil and often in clearings in
woods and along woods borders.
    USE. Like slimspike threeawn, this variety provides little forage for
cattle or wildlife.

9. Red threeawn *Aristida longiseta* Steud.
    Densely tufted perennial with stems 10–35 cm, and occasionally as
much as 50 cm, tall. *Leaves* usually short and in a dense tuft at the base of
the plant, but occasionally rather long and uniformly distributed on the
lower portion of the stems. *Sheaths* rounded on the back, downy on the
collar, and with tufts of long, soft hairs on either side of the collar. *Blades*
firm, inrolled from the edges, and 2 mm or less broad. In some forms, all
blades less than 8 cm long; in others, the blades to 15 cm long. *Inflorescences* narrow, bent or stiffly erect, contracted or open, and with slender,
spreading or drooping, few-flowered branches usually forming a panicle
but occasionally reduced to a three- to six-flowered raceme. *Spikelets* on
short or long stalks. *Glumes* broad, unequal, the first one-half to two-
thirds as long as the second and the second typically 16–25 mm long.
Lemmas mostly 13–15 mm long to the base of the awns, thick and straight

Fig. 9.   Red threeawn *(Aristida longiseta)* inflorescence and spikelet.

or slightly twisted above, without a well-defined neck or awn column. *Awns* nearly equal, mostly 4–10 cm long, relatively stout when 5 cm or less long. Plants producing seed mostly April to November, but occasionally collected in flower from March to December.

DISTRIBUTION AND HABITAT. Red threeawn occurs throughout the state except in the Pineywoods. It grows in heavily grazed pastures, on well-drained road and ditch banks, on dry, open slopes, and along washes.

USE. A widespread and common warm-season perennial of poor forage value for livestock and wildlife, red threeawn is frequent on sterile soils over a wide range and seems to intergrade with several other species of *Aristida*.

Fig. 10.   Oldfield threeawn *(Aristida oligantha)* plant.

10. Oldfield threeawn *Aristida oligantha* Michx.

Tufted annual with wiry, hairless, much-branched stems 15–80 cm tall. *Sheaths* rounded on the back and hairless or with a few hairs on either side of the collar. *Blades* hairless or sparsely stiff-haired above, with basal blades 10–25 cm long and 1–2 mm broad near the base, the upper blades short. *Inflorescence* a few-flowered, purplish panicle or raceme mostly 5–14 cm long, with large, widely spaced spikelets at the branch tips and on short, rough or downy stalks. *Glumes* narrowly lanceolate, nearly equal, mostly 18–25 mm long, the first usually three- to seven-nerved and awnless or short-awned and the second usually single-nerved, with an awn 1 cm or more in length from between two slender teeth 1–2 mm long. *Lemmas* slender, rough above, 16–28 mm long to the base of the awns, with a very short, poorly defined awn column. *Awns* abruptly spreading, 3–7 cm long, nearly equal or the central one longer. Plants producing seed mid-August to November.

DISTRIBUTION AND HABITAT. Oldfield threeawn is reported from all regions of Texas, but it is infrequent in the extreme eastern, southern, and northern portions of the state. A common and abundant weedy grass of the prairie regions of central and northern Texas, it is most common on sandy soils but also occurs on tight, clayey soils.

USE. This grass is essentially worthless as a forage grass, but it does have some value in protecting against erosion on loose-soiled disturbed and denuded sites. At maturity, oldfield threeawn seeds can give trouble by working their way into the wool of sheep and into the eyes of sheep and cattle.

11. Purple threeawn *Aristida purpurea* Nutt.

Low perennial with slender, tufted stems 25–70 cm tall. *Leaves* in a dense basal cluster or more frequently well distributed on the lower portion of the stems. *Sheaths* rough, hairless or minutely downy, and often with tufts of hair on either side of the collar. *Blades* variable, mostly 3–18 cm long and 0.7–2 mm broad, and typically inrolled, but the basal ones often remaining flat. *Panicles* 10–25 cm long, loosely or closely flowered but usually not appearing dense, the main axis bent or wavy and curving at maturity. *Panicle branches and spikelet stalks* slender, often threadlike, and spreading and curving under the weight of the mature grain but mostly erect when immature and after the panicles have shattered. *Glumes* unequal, the second mostly 11–15 mm long, as much as twice the length of the first. *Lemma* typically 10–12 mm long to the base of the awns, usually with rough lines, straight or slightly twisted above. *Awns* mostly 3.5–4.5 cm, occasionally up to 6 cm, long. Plants producing seed mostly April to October, but occasionally flowering throughout the year.

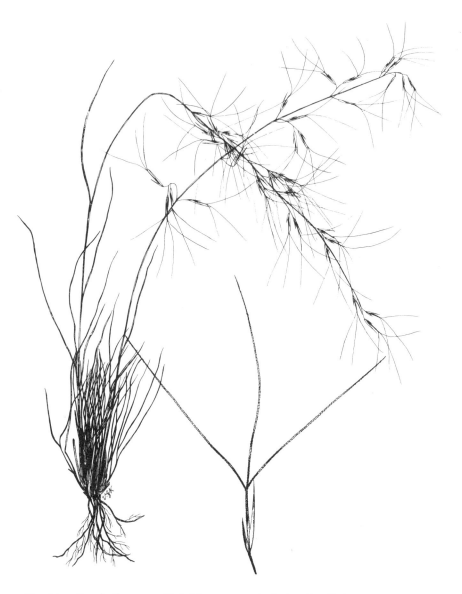

Fig. 11. Purple threeawn *(Aristida purpurea)* plant and spikelet.

DISTRIBUTION AND HABITAT. Purple threeawn is found throughout the state, except in the eastern Post Oak Savanna and Pineywoods, on both sandy and clayey soils, and it is frequent in almost solid stands on road rights of way in many areas.

USE. A grass mainly of overgrazed ranges, disturbed roadsides, and abandoned fields, purple threeawn is seldom grazed by livestock or wildlife and provides essentially no forage.

Fig. 12.   Roemer threeawn *(Aristida roemeriana)* plant and spikelet.

12. Roemer threeawn   *Aristida roemeriana* Scheele

Tufted perennial with numerous slender, erect stems mostly 25–70 cm tall. *Leaves* clustered at the base of the plant or scattered on the stems, hairless except for tufts of hair on either side of the collar. *Ligule* a small, fringed membrane to 0.6 mm long. *Blades* mostly 3–18 cm long

Fig. 13.   Wright threeawn *(Aristida wrightii)* plant, inflorescence, and spikelet.

and 0.7–2 mm broad, the broader ones often inrolled. *Panicles* 10–25 cm long and narrow but usually not appearing dense, the main axis wavy and curving at maturity, the branches and spikelet stalks slender and often spreading and curving under the weight of the mature grain. *Glumes* narrow and unequal, the first 3–6 mm long, half or less as long as the second. *Lemmas* 6–8 mm (occasionally up to 9 mm) long to the base of the awns, not twisted at the tip. *Awns* nearly equal, usually widely spreading, mostly 1.5–2.8 mm long but occasionally up to 3.5 cm long. Plants producing seed from early spring and throughout the summer and fall under favorable growing conditions.

DISTRIBUTION AND HABITAT. Roemer threeawn is frequent in sandy soils on the South Texas Plains and along the lower Gulf Prairies. It is gradually replaced to the north by the very similar but slightly more robust purple threeawn, which has slightly larger spikelets.

USE. Of little forage significance, Roemer threeawn is not grazed appreciably by livestock or wildlife.

13. Wright threeawn *Aristida wrightii* Nash

Tufted perennial with rather coarse stems mostly 35–80 cm tall. *Leaves* with a whitish waxy coating, distributed to well above the base. *Sheaths* rough, hairless or minutely downy, the collar often short-haired on the back and with tufts of long hairs on the sides. *Blades* firm, inrolled or mostly so, the lower ones 10–25 cm long and 1–2 mm broad, rough or roughly downy on the side toward the stem. *Panicles* contracted, 12–27 cm long, occasionally with rather long, stiff, and slightly spreading lower branches. *Glumes* unequal, the second 11–15 mm long and the first one-half to three-fourths as long. *Lemma* stout, with a thick, rough, straight or slightly twisted awn column equaling or slightly longer than the second glume. *Awns* mostly 15–30 mm long, with the central awn occasionally as much as 40 mm long. Plants producing seed mostly May to October, but occasionally as late as December.

DISTRIBUTION AND HABITAT. Found throughout the central and western portions of the state, Wright threeawn occurs on gravelly or sandy slopes and dry flats.

USE. A native, warm-season perennial that provides fair grazing for livestock and poor grazing for wildlife, Wright threeawn seldom is sufficiently abundant to provide a significant amount of forage.

ARUNDINARIA

14. Giant cane *Arundinaria gigantea* (Walt.) Muhl.

Shrubby perennial with woody stems 2–8 m tall from stout, creeping rhizomes. *Leaves* extremely variable in the development of sheath and blade, the lower leaves of the main shoots with reduced, often rudimen-

Fig. 14. Giant cane *(Arundinaria gigantea)* sterile shoot and inflorescences.

tary blades and short, broad sheaths that fall from the plant early. *Upper vegetative shoots* with blades 2–4 cm broad and 15–25 cm long, the flowering shoots with blades mostly 4 mm or less broad and 2–6 mm long. *Larger sheaths* with a hairy, elevated collar and auricles with usually 10–12 stiff bristles. *Larger blades* with a stalklike constriction at the base. *Inflorescences* on slender branches developed on the leafy stems or on specialized flowering stems produced directly from the rhizomes. *Inflorescences* with few to several large spikelets, the main axis terminating in a spikelet and the other spikelets stalked below. *Spikelets* 4–7 cm long, mostly with six to twelve flowers. *Glumes* widely separated, the first short, narrow, and developed, and the lowermost sometimes absent. *Lemmas* 1.5–2.5 cm long, mostly with seven to nine nerves, hairy at least near the base, and tapering to a point or a short awn at the apex. *Paleas* often nearly as large as the lemmas, rough on the nerves. Plants producing seed mostly in April and May at intervals of four to six years.

DISTRIBUTION AND HABITAT. Giant cane is frequent in low, moist woodlands and along streams and swales in the eastern and southeastern portions of the state.

USE. Giant cane is a good forage grass for both cattle and wildlife. It is grazed or browsed all year long, but it is especially valuable in Texas for cattle fodder during the winter and early spring months. Giant cane can be easily killed by overuse or by burning.

ARUNDO

15. Giant reed *Arundo donax* L.

Perennial with stout stems mostly 2–6 m tall from thick, knotty rhizomes, the plants often in dense colonies. *Leaves* hairless, rather uniformly spaced in two rows along the stem. *Blades* thick, flat, elongate, rough on the margins, the larger blades mostly 4–7 cm broad. *Inflorescence* a dense, contracted, many-flowered panicle 25–60 cm long, with numerous stiffly erect primary branches 15–25 cm or more long. *Spikelets* mostly with two to four flowers, 10–15 mm long, with short, hairless central axis joints. *Glumes* thin, long, nearly equal, irregularly with three or several nerves, narrowly pointed. *Lemmas* thin, with three to five nerves and long, soft hairs on the nerves, often short-awned at the pointed or slightly notched apex. Plants producing seed mostly September to November.

DISTRIBUTION AND HABITAT. Found throughout the state except on the High Plains, giant reed for the most part has been established through highway plantings along culverts and ditches and apparently does not produce fertile seed. It is an Old World species widely introduced in the southern United States.

Fig. 15.   Giant reed *(Arundo donax)* plant, spikelet, and floret.

USE. Giant reed is a poor forage grass for livestock or wildlife and is used very slightly by grazing or browsing animals when other food is available. This giant reed grass is most valuable in retarding erosion along ditches and stream banks, and it also provides cover for wild birds and small animals.

Fig. 16. Wild oat *(Avena fatua)* inflorescence and spikelet.

AVENA

16. Wild oat *Avena fatua* L.

Annual with hollow, weak stems and broad, flat blades. *Stems* hairless, mostly 30–120 cm tall. *Sheaths* hairless or with spreading hairs. *Ligule* a whitish membrane mostly 2–4 mm long, appearing as the continuation of the sheath margins. *Blades* flat, elongate, mostly 5–12 mm broad, hairless or fringed with hairs on the lower margins. *Inflorescence* a loose panicle or raceme with usually eight to thirty large, awned spikelets on slender curved or kinked stalks. *Spikelets* with usually three or four florets; when florets more than two, then the uppermost usually reduced and sterile. *Spikelet* breaking up above the glumes and between the florets. *Glumes* large, broad, hairless, narrowly pointed, with seven to nine nerves and broad, thin margins. *Lemmas* firm or hard, rounded, and with stiff, usually reddish brown hairs on the back, the lowermost lemma usually 1.5–2 cm long. *Awn of lemma* bent, mostly 2.5–4 cm long. *Paleas* thin, slightly shorter than the lemmas, with widely spaced, hairy nerves. Plants flowering March to June, but seldom producing seed.

DISTRIBUTION AND HABITAT. Wild oat is occasional in central and northern Texas as a weed of roadsides, ditches, and other areas of moist, disturbed soil. It is a European grass now present almost throughout the United States, except the Southeast, and is especially abundant along the coast of California.

USE. An introduced, cool-season annual, wild oat is leafy and palatable to livestock but short-lived and seldom abundant enough to provide significant amounts of forage.

Closely related to wild oat is the cultivated common oat (*Avena sativa* L.). This species has hairless lemmas, usually two-flowered spikelets, and lemma awns that are reduced, straight, or absent. Common oat is not infrequent on roadsides in areas where this cereal grass is cultivated as a crop plant.

AXONOPUS

17. Common carpetgrass *Axonopus affinis* Chase

Tufted perennial with mat-forming stolons and with laterally flattened stems and sheaths. *Stems* mostly from stolons, 20–70 cm tall, hairless or minutely downy on the nodes. *Leaves* hairless or margins of sheath and blade sparsely haired around the ligule. *Blades* rather thick, linear, 1.5–7 mm broad, abruptly pointed at the tip. *Inflorescence* with two to four slender, spikelike branches on a slender axis, the upper two branches usually paired at the apex of the stem. *Inflorescence branches* mostly 2.5–8 cm long, bearing two rows of spikelets closely pressed on a three-sided, slightly winged central stem. *Spikelets* mostly 1.8–2.6 mm long. *Glume and lemma of lower floret* sparsely hairy, narrowly ovate or oblong, flattened and nerveless in the middle, abruptly pointed at the apex, and slightly longer than the lemma of the upper floret. *Lemma of upper floret* minutely roughened, with thickened, inrolled margins. Plants producing seed mostly May to November.

DISTRIBUTION AND HABITAT. This species occurs in the eastern part of the state, mostly in moist, sandy openings in woods or along the borders of streams, lakes, and marshy areas.

USE. Common carpetgrass is a warm-season perennial that does well

Fig. 17.   Common carpetgrass *(Axonopus affinis)* plant and spikelet.

on relatively sterile soils and provides a fair amount of forage for livestock and wildlife.

BOTHRIOCHLOA

Key to the species:
Stalked spikelets neuter, smaller and narrower than the stalkless ones
    Stalkless spikelets less than 4.5 mm long; awn of lemma 18 mm or less
        long
        Panicles terminating the main stems 6–10 cm long; glumes relatively
           broad and blunt, dull green, commonly with a whitish waxy
           coating . . . . . . Silver bluestem, *B. saccharoides* var. *torreyana*
        Panicles terminating the main stems 10–20 cm long (late-produced
           stems often shorter); shiny green (southern and southeastern
           Texas) . . . .
        Longspike silver bluestem, *B. saccharoides* var. *longipaniculata*
    Stalkless spikelets 4.5–7.3 mm long; lemma awns 20–33 mm long . . .
        . . . . *B. barbinodis*
Stalked spikelets neuter or male (with stamens), about as large and broad
    as the stalkless ones . . . .
    . . . . King Ranch bluestem, *B. ischaemum* var. *songarica*

18. *Bothriochloa barbinodis* (Lag.) Herter
    Coarse perennial bunch grass, the stems erect or bent at the base, tending to become upward-curving and much-branched below in age, mostly 60–130 cm tall. *Stem nodes* bearded with hairs mostly 1–3 mm long, these typically erect and not widely spreading. *Leaves* usually hairless except for long hairs on the upper sheath margins and in the vicinity of the ligule. *Blades* firm, linear, 2–7 mm broad, often 25–30 cm or more long, but the upper blades greatly reduced. *Panicles* narrow, contracted, dense, mostly 7–13 cm long, often partially enclosed in the upper sheath, with a straight main axis and numerous primary branches mostly 4–9 cm long, these erect or loosely spreading at the tips; basal panicle branches moderately rebranched. *Internodes of panicle branches and spikelet stalks* more or less densely soft-haired on the thickened margins, with a broad, thin, membranous central region. *Stalkless spikelets* 4.5–7.3 mm long excluding the awns. *First glume* usually sparsely hairy below the middle. *Lemma awn* 20-30 mm or more long, bent and twisted.

Key to the varieties:
First (outer) glume of most or all stalkless spikelets without a glandular
    pit or depression . . . .
    . . . . Cane bluestem, *B. barbinodis* var. *barbinodis*
First (outer) glume of most stalkless spikelets with a glandular pit or de-
    pression at or above the middle . . . .
    . . . . Pinhole bluestem, *B. barbinodis* var. *perforata*

18a. **Cane bluestem** *Bothriochloa barbinodis* (Lag.) Herter var. *barbinodis* (*Andropogon barbinodis* Lag.)

Fig. 18.   Cane bluestem *(Bothriochloa barbinodis* var. *barbinodis)* inflorescence and spikelet pair, and pinhole bluestem *(Bothriochloa barbinodis* var. *perforata)* spikelet pair.

DISTRIBUTION AND HABITAT. This variety occurs in the western two-thirds of the state, mostly on loose, limey soils. Seed is set mostly May to October, but flowering occurs throughout the year under favorable growing conditions.

USE. Cane bluestem is a good forage grass for livestock, especially before the stems become fully mature and fibrous. Later in the season only the leaves are taken.

18b. Pinhole bluestem   *Bothriochloa barbinodis* (Lag.) Herter var. *perforata* (Trin. *ex* Fourn.) Gould
DISTRIBUTION AND HABITAT. With the same general distribution and

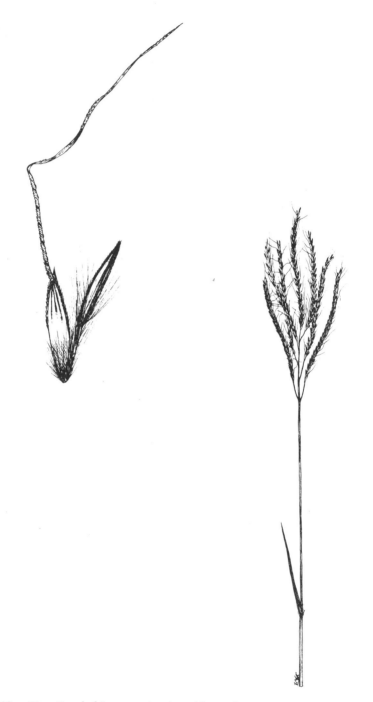

Fig. 19. King Ranch bluestem *(Bothriochloa ischaemum* var. *songarica)* inflorescence and spikelet pair.

40 : Common Texas Grasses

habitat preference as cane bluestem, pinhole bluestem flowers and fruits at the same time as the typical variety.

USE. Pinhole bluestem is a palatable forage grass with the same use as cane bluestem.

19. **King Ranch bluestem** *Bothriochloa ischaemum* (L.) Keng. var. *songarica* (Rupr.) Celerier & Harlan

Tufted perennial with slender, erect, or curving-erect stems developing both stolons and rhizomes under close grazing or cutting. *Stems* mostly 30–50 cm tall, but occasionally over 100 cm long when curved upward or trailing at the base. *Stem nodes* bearded with short hairs, the hairs often lost in age. *Sheaths* hairless and rounded. *Blades* linear, mostly 2–4 mm broad and 4–20 cm long, usually sparsely hairy with long, spreading hairs at least in the vicinity of the ligule. *Panicle* projecting well above the uppermost leaf, mostly 4–10 cm long and with two to eight, but occasionally only one, primary branches, the branches 3–9 cm long and only occasionally rebranched. *Panicle branches* slender and rounded below the spikelets. *Internodes of branch axis and spikelet stalks* fringed with hairs on margins, at least the uppermost with a narrow central groove. *Stalkless spikelets* 3–4.5 mm long and narrowly ovate. *First (outer) glume* never with a glandular pit or depression, usually rough on the margins and hairy on the back below the middle, the tip narrowly pointed. *Lemma awn* bent and twisted, mostly 1–1.5 cm long. *Stalked spikelet* with stamens only, awnless, about as long as the stalkless one but often slightly narrower. *First glume* hairless or hairy below the middle. Plants setting seed mostly July through November, but flowering throughout the year under favorable growing conditions.

DISTRIBUTION AND HABITAT. Found throughout the central portion of the state, King Ranch bluestem is a commonly seeded pasture grass that persists as a roadside grass throughout the area of distribution.

USE. This variety is a vigorous warm-season perennial that provides fair grazing for livestock and wildlife. King Ranch bluestem, now rather widespread in the southern United States, is native to Asia and Central Europe.

20. *Bothriochloa saccharoides* (Swartz) Rydb.

Strong perennial with stems in small to large bunches, never developing rhizomes or stolons. *Leaves and stems* green or with a whitish waxy coating, usually maturing with a bronze or reddish tinge. *Leaves* hairless except for a few long hairs in the vicinity of the ligule. *Blades* linear, firm, flat or irregularly folded, mostly 3–6 mm broad, and tapering to a long, slender tip. *Inflorescence* a densely flowered, contracted panicle, the branches erect or loosely erect and spreading with age. *Panicle branches* numerous, erect, pressed closely together, and shorter than the main axis. Branches and spikelet stalks with a thin central groove and thick margins fringed with long silky hairs. *Stalked spikelets* neuter, much narrower and usually shorter than the stalkless ones. *Glumes of stalkless spikelet* firm, the first flat on the back, larger than the second, and clasping it by the margins below the tip. *Second glume* broadly keeled. *Awn of lower floret* mostly 8–18 mm long, bent below the middle and with both segments loosely twisted.

Key to the varieties:

Panicles of larger stems 10–20 cm long; glume narrowly ovate and shiny green; southeastern and southern Texas . . . . Longspike silver bluestem, *B. saccharoides* var. *longipaniculata*
Panicles 6–10 (–13) cm long; glumes ovate, relatively broad and blunt, dull green, commonly with a whitish waxy coating; throughout the Texas range of the species . . . . Silver bluestem, *B. saccharoides* var. *torreyana*

20a. Longspike silver bluestem *Bothriochloa saccharoides* var. *longipaniculata* (Gould) Gould

Plants usually without a conspicuous basal cluster of leaves. *Stems* commonly 60–130 cm tall. *Leaves, stems, and spikelets* usually not with a whitish waxy coating. Flowering mostly May to November.

DISTRIBUTION AND HABITAT. Longspike silver bluestem occurs throughout eastern and southern Texas, mostly in openings in woods. It is well adapted to tight, clayey soils and is quite tolerant of shade.

USE. This variety is a relatively coarse-leaved perennial that grows well on poorer soils and provides good forage for livestock and fair forage for deer. Longspike silver bluestem seeds readily and is one of the first of the strong grass perennials to take over after the denudation of land because of soil disturbance or overgrazing.

20b. Silver bluestem *Bothriochloa saccharoides* var. *torreyana* (Steud.) Gould

Bunch grass with a conspicuous basal cluster of leaves and stems mostly 50–80 mm tall in small to moderately large clumps. *Leaves, stems, and spikelets* commonly hairless and with a whitish waxy coating.

DISTRIBUTION AND HABITAT. Silver bluestem is restricted to well-drained, usually sandy soils. On clayey soils it only grows on well-drained sites such as railroad and road embankments and dry banks of ditches and gulleys. It is present in all regions of the state, but it is less common in the eastern and coastal areas than is the longspike variety. In northern and western Texas it is a common perennial roadside grass. Its flowering period is mostly May to November.

Fig. 20a. Longspike silver bluestem (*Bothriochloa saccharoides* var. *lon-gipaniculata*) plant and spikelet pair.

Fig. 20b. Silver bluestem *(Bothriochloa saccharoides* var. *torreyana)* inflorescence and spikelet pair.

44 : Common Texas Grasses

USE. Silver bluestem is a native, warm-season perennial rated as fair for livestock and wildlife grazing. Although it is palatable to livestock during the growing period, this grass is only lightly used after it matures. It appears to be a good seeder on range sites, but the seedlings need protection from grazing to establish a stand.

BOUTELOUA

Key to the species:
Panicle branches breaking off as a whole, the spikelets falling with the
    main axis of the branch
    Panicle branches usually 20–50 or more ....
    .... Sideoats grama, *B. curtipendula* var. *curtipendula*
    Panicle branches mostly 2–15
        Spikelets closely spaced on the main axis of the branch, 1 mm or less
            apart; short-lived perennial ....
            .... Texas grama, *B. rigidiseta*
        Spikelets not closely spaced on the main axis of the branch, more
            than 1 mm apart; short-lived annual ....
            .... Needle grama, *B. aristidoides*
Panicle branches persistent, the spikelets breaking off at nodes above the
    glumes
    Plants annual .... Sixweeks grama, *B. barbata*
    Plants perennial
        Glumes and lemmas awnless ....
        .... (*See* buffalograss, *Buchloë dactyloides*)
        Glumes or lemmas short-awned
            Stem internodes, at least the lower ones, woolly ....
            ...., ... Black grama, *B. eriopoda*
            Stem internodes not woolly
                Inflorescence branches one to three, occasionally four; lower-
                  most (seed-bearing) floret with a tuft of hairs at its base, or
                  main axis of inflorescence branch projecting as a point well
                  beyond insertion of the terminal spikelet
                Main axis of inflorescence branch projecting as a point well
                  beyond insertion of the terminal spikelet; long hairs ab-
                  sent at the base of the perfect (lower) floret ....
                  .... Hairy grama, *B. hirsuta*
                Main axis of inflorescence branch not projecting as a point
                  beyond insertion of the terminal spikelet; tuft of long
                  hairs present at the base of the perfect floret ....
                  .... Blue grama, *B. gracilis*
                 Inflorescence branches three to eight; lowermost (seed-bearing)
                floret without a tuft of long hairs at its base; main axis of in-

Accounts of the Grasses : 45

florescence branch not projecting beyond insertion of the
terminal spikelet .... Red grama, *B. trifida*

Fig. 21.   Needle grama *(Bouteloua aristidoides)* plant and inflorescence branch
with two spikelets and lowermost spikelet.

21. Needle grama   *Bouteloua aristidoides* (H.B.K.) Griseb.

Tufted, short-lived annual with stems 6–50 cm or more long, the
outer stems curving erect from a spreading base. *Sheaths* usually much
shorter than the internodes. *Blades* short, thin, flat or folded, 1–2 mm
broad, and mostly hairless but often with a few long hairs at their base.
Inflorescences mostly 2.5–10 cm long, usually with four to fifteen short,
loosely spaced, and spreading branches that break off at a sharp-pointed
hairy basal callus when mature. *Inflorescence branches* mostly 1–2 cm

long and with one to four spikelets. *Branch axis* flattened, densely hairy at least near its base, the curved tip extended 5–10 mm beyond the attachment of the terminal spikelet. *Lowermost spikelet* closely pressed against the inflorescence central axis, usually without a rudiment and with an awnless or minutely awned lemma. *Upper spikelets* with a rudiment reduced to an awn column and three awns 2–6 mm long. *Glumes* very unequal, narrowly or broadly pointed, the larger one often spreading from the floret. *Lemma* about as long as the upper glume, with short or long awns. *Grains* brownish, narrow, flattened, mostly 2.5–3 mm long. Plants setting seed mostly August to October, but occasionally May to November.

DISTRIBUTION AND HABITAT. Needle grama occurs in the central and western portions of the state on dry, open slopes and along washes. It is frequent on graded roadsides.

USE. This species is a short-lived native annual of essentially no value as a forage grass. In some areas the "burs" (seed-bearing branches) of needle grama are a serious problem to the sheep industry because they stick in the wool and greatly reduce its value.

22. Sixweeks grama   *Bouteloua barbata* Lag.

Low, tufted annual with stems usually bent or curving upward from a spreading base. *Leaves* short, mostly basal, the sheaths rounded, with a tuft of long hairs on either side of the collar. *Blades* 1.5–7 cm long and 1–2 mm broad, flat or inrolled, often rough on the surface toward the stem and with a few long hairs just above the ligule. *Inflorescence* with three to seven persistent branches, these typically 1–3 cm long and with twenty-five to forty closely placed spikelets. *Spikelets* 2.5–4 mm long, including the short awns, usually with two reduced florets above the seed-bearing floret. *Glumes* hairless, the first 1.5–2 mm long and the second slightly longer, narrowly or broadly pointed or slightly notched and short-awned at the apex. *Axis of spikelet* with a tuft of silvery hairs below the lower rudimentary floret. *Lemma of lowermost (seed-bearing) floret* lobed and three-awned, the awns to 3 mm long. *Body of lemma* densely hairy, at least on the margins. *Lower rudimentary floret* with rounded lobes and three awns about as long as the lemma awns. *Upper rudimentary floret* reduced to a minute, inflated, awnless bract. Plants setting seed April to November.

DISTRIBUTION AND HABITAT. Frequent in the central, north-central, and western portions of the state, sixweeks grama is absent from the eastern Pineywoods and Post Oak Savanna. It occurs on dry, open, grassy rangeland, on roadsides, and in waste places, usually in sandy soils.

USE. Sixweeks grama is a native, short-lived annual with essentially no value as a forage grass.

Fig. 22. Sixweeks grama *(Bouteloua barbata)* plant.

23. Sideoats grama *Bouteloua curtipendula* (Michx.) Torr. var. *curtipendula*

 Strong perennial with stems mostly 40–90 cm tall, produced singly or in small clumps from stout creeping rhizomes. *Leaf blades* linear, usually 3–7 mm broad, bluish green, commonly hairless except for a few long, swollen-based hairs on the lower margins. *Inflorescence* a slender

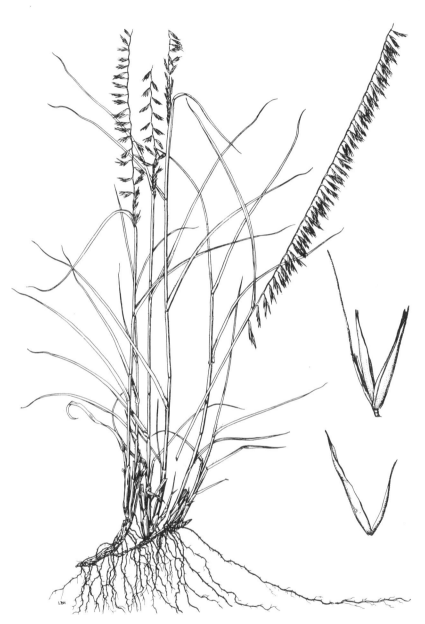

Fig. 23. Sideoats grama *(Bouteloua curtipendula* var. *curtipendula)* plant and spikelet with glumes separated from florets.

panicle with forty to seventy or more short, spikelike branches bent backwards along the stem, the branches each with three to seven stalkless spikelets and readily breaking off at maturity, leaving short basal stubs. *Spikelets* mostly 5–8 mm long, with a single seed-producing floret and a

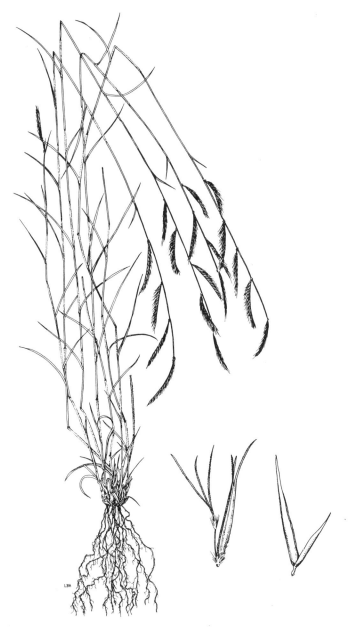

Fig. 24. Black grama *(Bouteloua eriopoda)* plant and spikelet with glumes separated from florets.

reduced floret above, the reduced floret neuter or occasionally with stamens only. *Second glume* as long as the spikelet, the first about two-thirds as long. *Lemmas* three-nerved, pointed or slightly three-toothed at the tip, the nerves extending into short awns. *Anthers* usually red or orange. Plants setting seed June through November.

DISTRIBUTION AND HABITAT. Sideoats grama is a widespread North American prairie grass present throughout Texas in open grasslands and along borders and openings of woods, rocky ridges, and road rights-of-way, usually in loamy, well-drained disturbed sites.

USE. This variety of grama grass is a native, warm-season perennial that provides good grazing for both livestock and wildlife. Along with its associated prairie grasses, sideoats grama provides an abundance of birdseed.

Of special interest in Texas is the relatively tall, coarse, bunch-grass type of sideoats that is frequent on loose soils in the southwestern part of the state. This grass, *Bouteloua curtipendula* var. *caespitosa* Gould & Kapadia, has not been given a common name, but selections of it have been given trade names. For the most part, the var. *caespitosa* is made up of plants that produce an abundance of good seed without fertilization of the egg cell.

24. Black grama *Bouteloua eriopoda* (Torr.) Torr.

Perennial with wiry, spreading stems mostly 20–60 cm long from a knotty base. Outer stems of a clump typically curving upward and often forming stolons that are woolly or downy on the lower internodes. *Leaves* short and inconspicuous, the sheaths much shorter than the internodes. *Blades* thin, flat or infolded, 0.5–2 mm broad, not producing much herbage. *Inflorescence* with three to eight slender, persistent, widely spaced flowering branches, these mostly 2–5 cm long and with eight to eighteen loosely spaced spikelets. *Branch axis* covered with dense white wool at its base and rough or inconspicuously hairy above. *Spikelets* with one seed-bearing floret and a single-awned rudiment above on a long stalk. *Glumes* unequal, hairless, narrowly or broadly pointed, the second mostly 6–9 mm long. *Lemmas* usually bearded at their base, otherwise hairless or sparsely covered with minute down, tapering above to a stout awn 1.5–3 mm long and much-reduced, bristle-like lateral awns. *Rudimentary floret* usually bearded at its base, with three awns 4–8 mm long. Plants setting seed June to October.

DISTRIBUTION AND HABITAT. Black grama is found in the central, north-central, and western regions of the state, mostly on gravelly uplands and often in association with shrubs and smaller woody plants on the more heavily grazed rangelands.

USE. A native, warm-season perennial that provides good grazing for both livestock and wildlife, black grama is eagerly sought by grazing animals, and under heavy grazing it persists only under the protection of shrubs. This grass is a good source of vitamin A during the winter months.

Fig. 25. Blue grama *(Bouteloua gracilis)* plant and spikelet with glumes separated from florets.

25. Blue grama *Bouteloua gracilis* (H.B.K.) Lag. *ex* Steud.

Tufted, sod-forming perennial, usually with short, stout rhizomes. *Stems* mostly 25–60 cm long, but occasionally much shorter, erect or somewhat bent at the base. *Sheaths* rounded, hairless or sparsely long-haired. *Blades* short, flat at their base, 1–2.5 mm broad, often sparsely hairy. *Inflorescences* with one to three or four branches, the branches 1.5–5 cm long. *Spikelets* closely placed and spreading, commonly forty to ninety or more per branch. *Branch axis* tipped by a spikelet, this usually reduced and often appearing as a continuation of the branch. *Spikelets* with one seed-producing floret and one or two rudimentary florets above. *Glumes* single-nerved and hairless or with swollen-based hairs on the midnerve. *Lemmas* mostly 4–5.5 mm long, hairy at least below, three-awned from a notched tip and lateral clefts, the awns mostly 1–3 mm long. *Base of lower (seed-producing) floret* and base of awned rudiment with a tuft of hair. *Second rudiment* (awnless) occasionally produced. Plants setting seed mostly June to October.

DISTRIBUTION AND HABITAT. Blue grama occurs in the northwestern, central, and western portions of the state on open, grassy plains and rocky slopes, growing best on loams and sandy loam soils.

USE. This grass is a native, warm-season perennial that provides good grazing for both livestock and wildlife. Blue grama withstands close grazing, but pastures in which it is the dominant grass should be rested every two or three years during the growing season. It cures well on the ground and occasionally is harvested for hay.

26. Hairy grama *Bouteloua hirsuta* Lag.

Tufted, short-lived perennial with weak, spreading or erect stems mostly 15–40 cm tall. *Stems* with four to six nodes, freely branching below. *Nodes* hairless. *Sheaths* hairless or the lowermost thinly soft-haired. *Blades* 1–2 mm broad, flat or infolded, and sparsely fringed on the lower margins with swollen-based hairs. *Inflorescence* 10–30 cm long, with one to four branches, these mostly 2.5–4 cm long and with twenty to fifty closely placed and spreading spikelets. *Branch axis* projecting as a point 5–8 mm or more beyond attachment of the terminal spikelet. *Spikelets* about 6 mm long. *Glumes* unequal, the first short and the second 3–5 mm long, with swollen-based hairs 1–2 mm long on the midnerve, minutely awned at the tip. *Lemma of seed-producing floret* 5–6 mm long, usually soft-haired on the back. *Rudimentary florets* two, the lower with three awns about 4 mm long and the upper a minute scale. *Spikelet axis* not hairy below the lower rudiment. *Grain* ovate, 1.5–2 mm long. Plants setting seed June to November.

DISTRIBUTION AND HABITAT. Hairy grama is found throughout the state, mostly on open, well-drained range sites and occasionally in open woodlands. It is adapted to a wide variety of soil types.

USE. Generally rated as a fair forage grass for both livestock and wildlife, hairy grama seldom is sufficiently abundant to be of much significance as a range forage grass. Typically, hairy grama has a weak root system and develops relatively little top growth.

Fig. 26. Hairy grama *(Bouteloua hirsuta)* plant.

54 : Common Texas Grasses

Fig. 27.   Texas grama *(Bouteloua rigidiseta)* plant and spikelet cluster.

27. Texas grama   *Bouteloua rigidiseta* (Steud.) Hitchc.

Tufted perennial with slender, weak stems, 15–50 cm tall, developed in small clumps. *Blades* narrow, flat or somewhat inrolled, mostly 4–15 cm long and 1–2 mm broad, and usually sparsely hairy. *Inflorescence main axis* 3–6 cm long above the lowermost branch. *Branches* wedge-shaped, mostly 0.8–1.6 cm long (including the awns), soon falling from

Fig. 28.   Red grama *(Bouteloua trifida)* plant and spikelet with glumes separated from florets.

56 : Common Texas Grasses

the main axis as a unit. Branches with three to five closely placed, spreading spikelets. *Branch axis* sparsely hairy, 4 7 mm long, deeply forked or divided into three points at the tip. *Spikelet* with one seed-bearing floret and one greatly reduced (rudimentary) floret. *Glumes* unequal, the second much larger than the first, with a closely appressed downy covering and with a stout midnerve that extends into a short, stout awn from between two thin, narrow, pointed lobes at the tip. *Lemma of seed-bearing floret* with a hairless or sparsely hairy body mostly 2.5–4 mm long, this divided above into two stout, short, spreading lateral awns and a slightly longer terminal awn extending from between the teeth of a notched tip. *Upper floret* rudimentary, usually reduced to an awn column and three awns 5–10 mm long. *Grain* flattened and narrowly obovate. Plants setting seed April to November under favorable conditions.

DISTRIBUTION AND HABITAT. Texas grama occurs throughout the state, except in the eastern Pineywoods and the extreme western portion, in grasslands, grassy openings in woods, and road rights-of-way, often on tight, clayey soils.

USE. A native, warm-season perennial that flowers relatively early in the spring, Texas grama has a weak root system and develops little herbage. It provides poor grazing for both livestock and wildlife.

28. Red grama *Bouteloua trifida* Thurb.

Densely tufted perennial with slender, wiry stems mostly 10–35 cm long, developed from a firm, often somewhat rhizomatous base. *Leaves* mostly in a basal clump, hairless or minutely hairy. *Blades* flat or loosely infolded. *Basal blades* mostly 4–8 cm long and 1.5 mm or less broad, the upper stem leaves greatly reduced. *Inflorescence* 3–9 cm long, with two to seven slender, persistent branches mostly 12–25 mm long and with eight to twenty-eight spikelets. *Lower floret of spikelet* seed-bearing, the upper floret an awned rudiment. *Glumes* slightly unequal, hairless, narrowly pointed or short-awned from a slightly notched tip. *Body of lemma* about 2 mm long, hairless or minutely hairy at the base, the hairs not over 0.5 mm long. *Awn of lower lemma* about twice as long as the body. *Rudimentary floret* with a short awn column and awns mostly 3.5–6 mm long. Plants setting seed mostly April to November, but flowering whenever growing conditions are favorable.

DISTRIBUTION AND HABITAT. Red grama is reported from all regions except the easternmost and southernmost parts of the state and is most frequent in the west. It grows mostly on clay or gravelly clay.

USE. A native, warm-season perennial of poor grazing value for both livestock and wildlife, red grama persists on poor soils and under heavy grazing pressures. It has considerable value as a soil binder in many areas of the west.

Plants of red grama flowering the first year are sometimes confused with the annual sixweeks grama. The latter has a conspicuously hairy lemma, relatively short lemma awns, and spreading stems curving out and upward from the base.

BRACHIARIA

Key to the species:
Spikelets densely hairy on the margins; perennial . . . .
. . . . Fringed signalgrass, *B. ciliatissima*
Spikelets hairless or sparsely hairy; annuals
    Spikelets 2.4–3 mm long . . . . Browntop brachiaria, *B. fasciculata*
    Spikelets 4 mm or more long
        Spikelets 4–4.5 mm long; branch axis 1.6–2.3 mm broad . . . .
        . . . . Broadleaf signalgrass, *B. platyphylla*
        Spikelets 5–6 mm long; branch axis less than 1.6 mm broad . . . . . .
        . . . . Texas brachiaria, *B. texana*

29. Fringed signalgrass *Brachiaria ciliatissima* (Buckl.) Chase
    Low perennial with erect stems mostly 15–40 cm tall, produced singly or in small clumps at the nodes of long, freely branched stolons. *Sheaths* variously hairy with long and short spreading hairs. *Blades* short, flat, rough, narrowly to broadly pointed at the tip, 2–7 mm broad and 3–8 cm long. *Panicle* few-flowered, 3–7 cm long, with short erect or spreading branches, these spikelet-bearing to their bases. *Spikelets* 3.5–4.5 mm long, awnless. *First glume* pointed, hairless, three-fourths as long as the spikelet. *Second glume and lemma of lower floret* about equal, five-nerved, densely hairy on the margins and downy with short, fine hairs on the back. *Lemma and palea of upper floret* firm, finely roughened. Plants setting seed mostly April to June, occasionally July to November.
    DISTRIBUTION AND HABITAT. Fringed signalgrass occurs in sandy soils throughout the state except in the extreme western portion.
    USE. This species is a fair forage grass for livestock and wildlife where it is developed in large stands. Perhaps the greatest value of fringed signalgrass is as a soil binder and sand dune stabilizer.

30. Browntop brachiaria *Brachiaria fasciculata* (Sw.) S. T. Blake
    (*Panicum fasciculatum* Swartz)
    Tufted annual with stems 30–120 cm or more long, these often curving upward from a reclining base and rooting at the nodes. *Stems and leaves* usually more or less hairy. *Blades* flat, mostly 4–20 cm long and 5–15 mm broad, narrowing slightly at the base and gradually tapering to a point at the tip. *Panicles* 6–15 cm long, with closely pressed or spreading, mostly simple branches 1–8 cm long. *Branchlets and short spikelet stalks*

Fig. 29.   Fringed signalgrass (*Brachiaria ciliatissima*) plant and inflorescence.

Fig. 30. Browntop brachiaria (*Brachiaria fasciculata*) plant, spikelet, and floret.

Fig. 31. Broadleaf signalgrass *(Brachiaria platyphylla)* plant and spikelet.

usually rough or downy and with a few to numerous long, stiff, silvery hairs, these occasionally absent. *Spikelets* hairless, broadly rounded, mostly 2.4–3 mm long but occasionally shorter, and usually yellowish brown or bronze colored. *First glume* thin, one-fourth to one-third as long as the spikelet. *Second glume and lower lemma* usually with fine cross-veins to well below the middle, rounded or slightly pointed at the tip. *Lemma of upper floret* rough, nearly as long as the spikelet, the tip blunt, not abruptly pointed or beaked. Plants setting seed mostly June to November, but occasionally in April or May.

DISTRIBUTION AND HABITAT. Reported from all areas of the state except the Pineywoods, browntop brachiaria is a weedy plant of low, moist sites and is often found in ditches, low fields, graded roadsides, and waste places.

USE. This tropical annual is generally reported as introduced, but it may be native. It has no forage significance, but it probably has considerable value in supplying birdseed in the moist habitats.

31. Broadleaf signalgrass *Brachiaria platyphylla* (Griseb.) Nash

Coarse annual with stems curving upward from spreading bases, these rooting at the lower nodes. *Sheaths* hairless or sparsely hairy, fringed with hairs on the upper margins. *Blades* hairless on both surfaces, mostly 6–13 mm broad. *Inflorescence* of two to six unbranched, widely spaced, erect or somewhat spreading branches. *Branches* 3–6 cm long, with a flattened, winged main axis 1.6–2.3 mm broad. *Spikelets* 4–4.5 mm long, ovate, hairless. *First glume* one-fourth to one-third as long as the spikelet. *Second glume and lemma of lower floret* about equal, with strong cross-veinlets at least near the tip, usually extended 0.8–1.2 mm beyond the tip of the upper floret. *Lemma and palea of upper floret* firm, finely roughened, the lemma with thick, inrolled margins. Plants setting seed April to November.

DISTRIBUTION AND HABITAT. Broadleaf signalgrass is occasional in the eastern, central, and southern regions of the state along openings in woods, swales, ditches, field borders, and other areas of moist soil.

USE. This native annual is not significant as a forage grass, although the herbage is succulent and tender. It is primarily a casual weed of moist, disturbed soils.

32. Texas brachiaria (Texas millet) *Brachiaria texana* (Buckl.) S. T. Blake (*Panicum texanum* Buckl.)

Coarse-leaved annual, frequently forming large clumps. *Stems* mostly 40–120 cm or more tall or long, commonly curving upward from a spreading base or creeping and rooting at the lower nodes, with soft down at least on and just below the nodes. *Leaves* usually hairy with short or long hairs, occasionally nearly hairless. *Blades* lanceolate, firm, flat or

Fig. 32.   Texas brachiaria *(Brachiaria texana)* inflorescence and spikelet.

folded, mostly 8–20 cm long and 7–20 mm broad, usually covered on both surfaces with short, fine, soft hairs. *Panicles* 7–18 cm, and occasionally up to 25 cm, long, with short, usually simple, erect or slightly spreading branches. *Panicle branches and spikelet stalks* usually densely covered with fine down and with a few long, silvery, stiff hairs. *Spikelets* 5–6 mm long, often sparsely downy. *First glume* about two-thirds as long as the spikelet, with five to seven strong nerves. *Second glume and lower lemma* with five strong nerves, about equal. *Lower floret* with stamens only and with a thin, silvery palea about as long as the lemma. *Lemma and palea of upper floret* transversely roughened, the lemma slightly beaked, mostly 3.5–4 mm long. Plants setting seed late May to November.

DISTRIBUTION AND HABITAT. Texas brachiaria is distributed throughout the state except in the far west and the extreme northwest. It is a weedy species of ditches, field borders, vacant lots, and other areas of moist, disturbed soils.

USE. This grass is a native, warm-season annual growing mainly as a weed of cultivated fields, moist ditches, and vacant lots. It is of little or no significance as a range forage grass.

BRIZA

33. Little quakinggrass *Briza minor* L.

Delicate, short-lived annual with stems single or in small clumps, mostly 15–50 cm tall. *Leaves and stems* hairless or essentially so. *Blades* thin, flat, mostly 2–8 mm broad and 4–18 cm long, gradually merging into the sheath on the back surface. *Panicles* 3–15 cm long, typically much-branched and open, with small, awnless spikelets on long, slender, spreading, usually kinked stalks. *Spikelets* 3–6 mm long and about as broad, hairless, with three to twelve flowers. *Glumes* longer than the successively shorter lemmas, the spikelet somewhat pyramid-shaped. *Lemmas* indistinctly nerved, with a firm, shiny central portion and broad, thin margins. *Grain* light brown, rounded, flattened on one side, mostly 0.6–0.8 mm long. Plants setting seed in April and May.

DISTRIBUTION AND HABITAT. This species is occasional and often locally abundant in moist woodland clearings and along semidisturbed soils of roadsides and ditch banks in eastern Texas.

USE. A low, short-lived, native annual with no forage significance, this grass appears early in the spring, commonly in association with common sixweeksgrass (*Vulpia octoflora*), little barley (*Hordeum pusillum*), and Japanese brome (*Bromus japonicus*).

Fig. 33.   Little quakinggrass *(Briza minor)* inflorescence.

Fig. 34.   Japanese brome *(Bromus japonicus)* inflorescence and spikelet.

BROMUS

Key to the species:

Spikelets with awns 8 mm or more long; spikelets not laterally flattened
and not keeled on the lemma midnerves

First glume with one and occasionally with three nerves; lemma awns
12–18 mm long . . . . Downy brome, *B. tectorum*

First glume with three to five nerves; lemma awns 8–13 mm long . . .
. . . . Japanese brome, *B. japonicus*

Spikelets awnless or the lemmas with awn tips less than 4 mm long;
spikelets flattened laterally and sharply keeled on the lemma mid-
nerves . . . . Rescuegrass, *B. unioloides*

34. Japanese brome *Bromus japonicus* Thunb.

Annual with slender, weak stems mostly 30–60 cm tall. *Sheaths*, at
least the lowermost, typically hairy, with the hairs matted, spreading, or
bent backwards. *Blades* usually hairy, 2–7 mm broad. *Panicles* 8–20 cm
long, with slender, wavy and often kinked branches and spikelet stalks,
these spreading from the main axis and curving or erect at maturity.
Spikelets 1.5–3 cm long, excluding the awns, with six to eleven florets.
Glumes broad, hairless, and awnless, the first with three to five nerves
and the second with five to nine nerves. *Lemmas* hairless, awned, mostly
7–9 mm long, rounded on the back, with thin, flat margins and thin,
pointed teeth mostly 1.5–2 mm long at the tip. *Awn of lemma* slender,
straight or wavy, and 8–13 mm long. Plants setting seed March to May.

DISTRIBUTION AND HABITAT. Reported from all regions of Texas except
the eastern Pineywoods, Japanese brome is a common introduced weed of
roadsides, field borders, and pastures.

USE. Japanese brome frequently occurs in dense stands along roadside ditches, where it may have some value as a soil stabilizer. It has no
significance as a range forage grass.

35. Downy brome (downy chess; cheatgrass) *Bromus tectorum* L.

Annual with weak erect or spreading stems usually 25–60 cm tall.
Sheaths and blades usually softly hairy but occasionally hairless or nearly
so. *Blades* typically 2.5–6 mm broad. *Panicles* narrow and loosely contracted, the branches and spikelet stalks slender, bent, and often
S-curved. *Spikelets* mostly 1.2–2 cm long, excluding the awns, and usually with four to six florets. *Glumes* unequal, thin, and pointed, with
broad, translucent margins, the first with one to three nerves and the
second three-nerved, often notched at the tip. *Lemmas* mostly 9–12 mm
long, with thin, membranous margins and slender teeth 2–3 mm long at
the tip. *Lemma awns* 12–18 mm long. Plants setting seed in spring and
early summer.

Fig. 35. Downy brome *(Bromus tectorum)* plant and spikelet.

DISTRIBUTION AND HABITAT. Downy brome is a short-lived weedy annual of heavily grazed rangelands, roadsides, and other open, disturbed sites from the Cross Timbers and Edwards Plateau westward. It is adventive in the United States from Europe and is now common throughout most of the country except the Southeast.

68 : Common Texas Grasses

USE. Downy brome is an introduced, relatively unpalatable, short-lived annual that has become abundant throughout large areas of rangeland in the western United States. When growing in large stands, it does provide forage for sheep in the spring and also has value in erosion control on denuded slopes. With good range management practices, downy brome tends to be replaced by the more valuable perennial grasses.

36. Rescuegrass *Bromus unioloides* (Willd.) H.B.K.

Tufted annual (in Texas), with stems mostly 50–80 cm tall. *Young shoots* soft and succulent, laterally flattened and usually somewhat keeled. *Sheaths* nearly hairless to densely hairy with fine, straight, spreading hairs. *Blades* mostly 5–12 mm broad, hairless or hairy, with a yellowish band just above the ligule. *Inflorescence* an open, drooping panicle of large, flattened spikelets, these mostly 2–3 cm long and with six to twelve florets. *Glumes* awnless, the first usually with five to seven nerves and the second usually with seven to nine nerves. *Lemmas* with seven to eleven nerves, laterally flattened and sharply keeled, hairless or variously hairy, awnless or with an awn 1–3 mm long. Plants setting seed mostly February to May. This is one of the first of the cool-season grasses to flower in the spring.

DISTRIBUTION AND HABITAT. Found in all regions of Texas, rescuegrass was introduced into the western United States from South America as a forage grass but is now growing mostly as a weed of ditches, vacant lots, old fields, and roadsides.

USE. Rescuegrass provides a relatively small amount of forage on ranges and is rated as fair for grazing livestock and wildlife. It reproduces from seed and is grown as a cool-season pasture plant.

BUCHLOË

37. Buffalograss *Buchloë dactyloides* (Nutt.) Engelm.

Low, mat-forming perennial with extensive wiry stolons and tufted leaves. *Sheaths* rounded on the back and hairless except for a few marginal hairs in the vicinity of the collar. *Blades* flat, hairless or thinly hairy on one or both surfaces, mostly 1–2.5 mm broad, commonly 2–15 cm long but occasionally longer. Male and female flowers borne on separate plants, the male inflorescences resembling those of blue grama, but much smaller, and the female inflorescences in tight little heads or burs. *Male inflorescences* elevated above basal leaves on slender, erect stems mostly 8–25 cm tall, with one to four spikelike, one-sided branches mostly 6–14 mm long. *Main axis* of flowering branch narrow, flattened, bearing usually six to twelve closely placed spikelets, these mostly 4–5.5 mm long. *Male spikelets* two-flowered, both flowers anther-bearing, with broad, unequal glumes that are shorter than the lemmas. *Lemmas* of male

Fig. 36.   Rescuegrass *(Bromus unioloides)* plant, spikelet, and floret.

Fig. 37. Buffalograss *(Buchloë dactyloides)*. *Below:* male (staminate) plant and male spikelet with glumes separated from floret. *Above:* female (pistillate) plant, flowering branch, spikelet cluster, and floret.

spikelets thin, three-nerved, typically hairless and awnless. *Female spikelets* single-flowered, in burlike clusters of three to five, occasionally to seven, and more or less hidden in the leafy portion of the plant. *Bur* on a short, stout stalk, partially enclosed in a broad, reduced leaf sheath, falling as a unit, with the stalk fused to the hard second glume of the spikelets. *Glumes* of female spikelets unequal, the first usually reduced, the second broad and hard below, abruptly narrowing to three stiff, pointed lobes. *Lemmas* of female spikelets thin but firm, hairless, three-nerved, the nerves extending into short, awn-tipped lobes. Grain ovate or oblong, brownish, mostly 2–2.5 mm long. Plants setting seed April to December under favorable growing conditions.

DISTRIBUTION AND HABITAT. Buffalograss is occasional in all regions of the state, but it is most frequent in short-grass prairies, heavily grazed tall-grass regions, and mowed roadsides of the central and north-central portions of Texas. It is adapted best to loamy clay soils subject to runoff water during rainy periods. It is very hardy and persists under long summer droughts and long periods of flooding.

USE. This grass is a low, sod-forming, native perennial that provides good grazing for livestock and fair grazing for wildlife.

CALAMOVILFA

38. Big sandreedgrass *Calamovilfa gigantea* (Nutt.) Scribn. & Merr.

Large, coarse perennial with stout, creeping rhizomes. *Stems* mostly solitary at the nodes of the rhizomes, usually 1–2 m tall and 4–15 mm or more thick near the base. *Sheaths* rounded and hairless or occasionally minutely downy near the collar. *Blades* elongate, firm, hairless, flat or folded, 5–12 mm broad near their base, and tapering to a long, narrow, infolded tip. *Panicles* large and open, mostly 30–60 cm long and with stiffly ascending or spreading branches to 20 cm or more long, the longer branches bare of spikelets or secondary branches on the lower 2.5–6 cm. *Spikelets* one-flowered, awnless, mostly 7–10 mm long, clustered at the branch tips on very short stalks, and breaking up above the glumes. *Glumes* firm or papery, hairless, single-nerved, pointed, the second equaling or exceeding the lemma and the first slightly shorter. *Lemma* similar to the glumes in texture, single-nerved, narrow above, pointed at the tip, downy on the back below the middle, and with a tuft of silvery hairs 3–5 mm long at the base. *Palea* narrow, usually slightly longer than the lemma and of similar texture, downy on the nerves below the middle. Plants flowering mostly June to October.

DISTRIBUTION AND HABITAT. This species is a grass of deep sandy sites in the more arid region of western Texas.

USE. Big sandreedgrass is mainly of value in controlling wind erosion on deep sands that tend to develop dunes. This grass cures well in the field and provides good winter forage for livestock where it is sufficiently abundant.

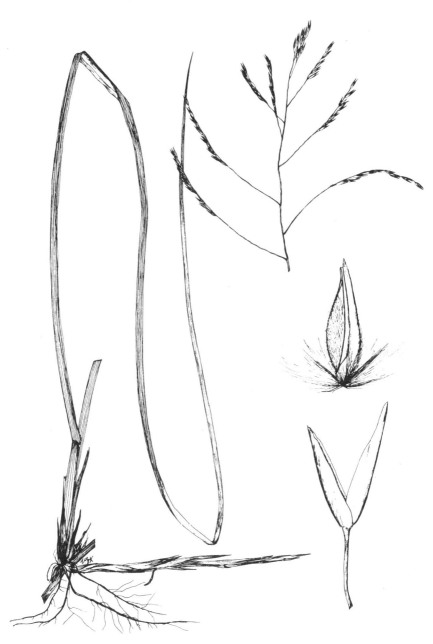

Fig. 38.   Big sandreedgrass *(Calamovilfa gigantea)* plant base, inflorescence, and spikelet with glumes separated from floret.

CENCHRUS

Key to the species:

Burs with stout, flattened, barbed spines, the spines projecting at irregular intervals throughout the body of the bur; annual or weak perennial .... Sandbur, *C. incertus*

Burs without stiff, flattened spines; plants perennial

  Burs conspicuously long-haired .... Buffelgrass, *C. ciliaris*

  Burs roughened with short prickle-hairs ....

  .... Big cenchrus, *C. myosuroides*

39. Buffelgrass *Cenchrus ciliaris* L.

Tufted perennial with stems erect or spreading from a branched and "knotty" base and 50–100 cm tall. *Sheaths* laterally compressed and keeled, hairless to sparsely covered with soft, straight hairs. *Blades* thin, usually flat, rough or slightly soft-haired, mostly 8–30 cm long and 2.5–8 mm broad. *Inflorescence* a dense, cylindrical panicle mostly 4–10 cm long and 1–2 cm thick. *Bristles* of the "bur" 4–10 mm long, purplish, long-haired on their inner margins, rounded, fused together only at their base or to slightly above the base. *Bur* containing two to four spikelets, readily breaking off at the base of the minute, soft-haired stalk at maturity. *Spikelets* 2.2–5.6 mm long. *Grain* swollen, ovoid, 1.4–1.9 mm long, about 1 mm in diameter. Plants setting seed from early spring until late autumn under favorable growing conditions.

DISTRIBUTION AND HABITAT. This species is an introduced grass now common in sandy soils on rangelands, old fields, and other semidisturbed sites throughout the South Plains and also occasional in the central and western parts of the state. It is native to India and Africa.

USE. Buffelgrass is a good forage grass for both livestock and wildlife.

40. Sandbur (grassbur) *Cenchrus incertus* M. A. Curtis

Annual or short-lived perennial with weak, erect or abruptly bent and spreading stems mostly 8–80 cm long. *Sheaths* laterally compressed, hairless or sparsely soft-haired. *Blades* thin, flat, typically hairless, mostly 2–18 cm long and 2–6 mm broad. *Inflorescence* a contracted cluster of spiny burs on an angular axis 1.5–8 cm long. *Burs* variable, ovoid to round, with clefts on two sides. *Barbed spines* eight to forty per bur, irregularly protruding from the body, variable in shape, 2–5 mm long, 0.7–2 mm broad at the usually flattened base. *Spikelets* two to four, usually three, per bur, mostly 3.5–5.8 mm long. Plants setting seed mostly summer and fall.

DISTRIBUTION AND HABITAT. Found throughout the state, the sandbur is a common weed of pastures, roadsides, ditches, vacant city lots, weedy lawns, and other areas of disturbed soils. It occurs mostly in sand but also in clayey soils.

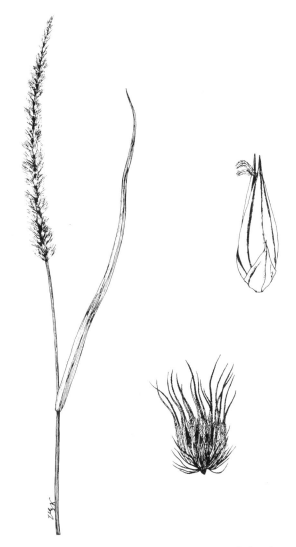

Fig. 39. Buffelgrass *(Cenchrus ciliaris)* inflorescence, spikelet cluster (bur), and spikelet.

USE. Sandbur is an annoying weed that often persists in improved pastures after they have been seeded to perennial grasses. It is of no forage value.

41. Big cenchrus (big sandbur) *Cenchrus myosuroides* H.B.K.
Coarse bunch grass with stout stems in large clumps. *Stems* more or

Fig. 40.　Sandbur *(Cenchrus incertus)* plant, bur, and spikelet.

76 : Common Texas Grasses

Fig. 41. Big cenchrus (*Cenchrus myosuroides*) inflorescence and spikelet cluster (bur).

less woody, mostly 0.7–2 m tall, little-branched above the base, with slightly swollen nodes. *Blades* rough at least on the surface facing the stem, occasionally slightly hairy, mostly 12–40 cm long and 4–13 mm broad, flat or somewhat folded. *Inflorescence* dense, cylindrical, 8–20 cm long and 6–12 mm thick. *Burs* with rounded spines and bristles, the bristles not flattened or barbed but with rough hairs, the inner bristles about as long as the spikelet and the outer ones shorter, irregular in length. *Bristles of bur* fused below into a hard, conical base that readily breaks off. *Spikelets* usually only one per bur, mostly 4–5 mm long. Plants setting seed May through November.

DISTRIBUTION AND HABITAT. Big cenchrus grows on sandy or clayey flats and lowlands in the South Plains, on the Edwards Plateau, and in western Texas.

USE. A native, perennial, warm-season grass that provides good grazing for livestock and fair grazing for wildlife, big cenchrus is a good grass for rangelands where only cattle are to be grazed, but it decreases in stand with heavy grazing. The burs cling to wool and mohair.

Fig. 42. Longleaf chasmanthium (*Chasmanthium latifolium*) plant, spikelet, and floret.

78 : Common Texas Grasses

CHASMANTHIUM

42. Longleaf chasmanthium *Chasmanthium latifolium* (Michx.) Yates

Slender perennial with stems up to 1.5 m tall from a knotty or some-what rhizome-forming base. *Nodes* hairless, often reddish purple. *Leaves* hairless, or essentially so, the blades thin and flat, mostly 1–2 cm broad, gradually narrowing at both ends. *Inflorescence* typically a panicle, but occasionally a raceme, with large, flattened, many-flowered, awnless spikelets borne on slender stalks. *Spikelets* mostly with six to twenty flowers, about 1 cm broad and 2–5 cm long. *Glumes and lemmas* sharply keeled and laterally compressed. *Lower one or two florets* steril. *Glumes* small, pointed, nearly equal, with five to seven nerves. *Lemmas* with eleven to fifteen nerves. *Grain* 2–2.5 mm wide, 3–5 mm long, brown to reddish black or black. Plants setting seed mostly June to October.

DISTRIBUTION AND HABITAT. Longleaf chasmanthium grows in moist, shaded, woodland habitats and along streambanks throughout the eastern and central portions of the state, but it is absent from the South Texas Plains and western Texas.

USE. This grass is a native, warm-season perennial that provides good forage for livestock and wildlife when in significant stands.

CHLORIS

Key to the species:

Florets three or four, only the lowermost seed-bearing, the upper ones
progressively reduced . . . . Rhodesgrass, *C. gayana*
Florets two, the lower one seed-bearing, the upper one large or reduced but never seed-bearing
Panicle branches in a single whorl, or if in several whorls, then
crowded near the tip of the panicle . . . .
. . . . Hooded windmillgrass, *C. cucullata*
Panicle branches irregularly in several whorls along 20 mm or more
of the inflorescence axis . . . . Windmillgrass, *C. verticillata*

43. Hooded windmillgrass *Chloris cucullata* Bisch.

Tufted perennial with flattened, leafy basal shoots and stems 15–60 cm tall. *Sheaths* and even the blades folded on the midnerve, the sheaths laterally flattened. *Leaves* hairless, up to 20 cm long and 2–4 mm broad. *Panicles* with ten to twenty spreading branches 2–5 cm long, these crowded in one or several close whorls. *Spikelets* at first straw-colored, later becoming brownish, closely spaced and widely divergent, with about fourteen to eighteen spikelets per centimeter of central axis length. *Glumes* lanceolate to obovate, hairless, unequal, the first short, the second 1–1.5 mm long. *Lemma* of lowermost floret 1.5–2 mm long, with an

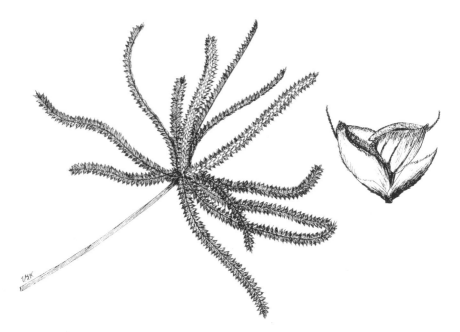

Fig. 43.   Hooded windmillgrass *(Chloris cucullata)* inflorescence and spikelet.

awn 0.3–1.5 mm long from a blunt tip. *Upper floret* conspicuously swollen, with the upper margins inrolled, 1–1.5 mm long, unawned or with an awn up to 1.5 mm long. Plants setting seed May through September.

DISTRIBUTION AND HABITAT. Frequent in the central and western portions of the state, mainly in pastures, lawns, parks, and vacant lots, hooded windmillgrass grows mainly in acid to neutral soils of medium to coarse texture.

USE. This grass is a native, warm-season perennial that provides fair grazing for livestock and wildlife.

44. Rhodesgrass   *Chloris gayana* Kunth

Leafy perennial with stems tufted from stout, creeping rhizomes. *Erect stems* mostly 80–100 cm tall, occasionally taller. *Leaves* hairless, the blades flat and somewhat thickened, linear, up to 30 cm long and 1.5 cm broad. *Panicle* with nine to thirty branches clustered at the tip, the branches mostly 8–12 cm long. *Spikelets* closely placed, pale or tawny. *Glumes* narrowly pointed, hairless, the first glume 1.4–2.8 mm long and the second 2.5–4.3 mm long. *Lemma of lower (seed-bearing) floret* with a body mostly 2.5–4.5 mm long, the upper margins usually with a tuft of short hairs. *Reduced florets* usually two to four, rarely one, similar to the lower floret but progressively smaller, the uppermost often minute. Plants setting seed May through December.

Fig. 44. Rhodesgrass *(Chloris gayana)* plant and spikelet.

DISTRIBUTION AND HABITAT. Rhodesgrass is an important cultivated grass of South Texas and the Gulf Coast, frequently growing along roads, in ditches, and in waste places, mostly in loamy soils. It probably is native to Africa.

USE. This introduced perennial is highly valued as forage grass, but it is established only to a limited extent out of cultivation.

45. Windmillgrass *Chloris verticillata* Nutt.

Perennial with shoot bases flattened and often curving upward or forming stolons, the stems 15–40 cm tall. *Leaves and stems* hairless, the sheaths laterally flattened, the blades narrow, mostly 2–3 mm broad and 8–15 cm long. *Panicle* with ten to sixteen slender, spreading branches 5–15 cm long, arranged in two to five whorls, these often separated by 5 mm or more. Panicle axis usually tipped by a single upright branch. *Spikelets* widely spaced on and pressed against the branches, with usually four to seven spikelets per centimeter of central axis length. *Spikelets* two-flowered, the lower floret seed-bearing and the upper floret neuter and reduced in size. *Glumes* lanceolate, membranous, hairless, the first glume 2–3 mm long and the second 2.8–3.5 mm long. *Lemma of lower floret* 2–3.5 mm long, with a hairless keel and hairy margins, the tip pointed or rounded, with an awn 4.8–9 mm long. Upper floret short and somewhat inflated, hairless, 1.1–2.3 mm long with an awn 3.2–7 mm long. Plants setting seed May through September.

DISTRIBUTION AND HABITAT. Windmillgrass occurs in the northern, central, and western parts of the state in heavy sandy or gravelly soils of disturbed areas, roadsides, lawns, and parks.

USE. This species is a native, warm-season perennial that provides poor grazing for both livestock and wildlife.

Windmillgrass hybridizes extensively with hooded windmillgrass (*Chloris cucullata*), and where the two grow together, they often form extensive populations of intermediate plants.

COELORACHIS

46. Carolina jointtail *Coelorachis cylindrica* (Michx.) Nash

Tufted perennial with or without rhizomes and with narrow, flat blades. *Stems and leaves* hairless, the stems mostly 30–100 cm tall. *Blades* flat or folded, mostly 8–30 cm long and 1.5–4 mm broad. *Inflorescence* a cylindrical or flattened spikelike raceme with short, stout, club-shaped internodes. *Raceme* slender, hairless, 6–15 cm long, well projecting from or enclosed at the base by the upper sheath, breaking apart at the central axis nodes. *Spikelets* awnless, in pairs of one stalkless and seed-bearing and one stalked, reduced, and neuter (in our species). *Stalkless spikelets* 4–6 mm long, rounded on the back. *Lower glume* firm or hard, usually winged, double-keeled below, and rough or pitted on the back at least on the margins (in our species). *Lemmas of both lower and upper florets* of stalkless spikelet thin, translucent, and awnless. *Plants* setting seed mostly May to July, but occasionally flowering in summer and autumn.

DISTRIBUTION AND HABITAT. This grass grows throughout all but the far western and northwestern parts of Texas and is widespread in tall-grass

Fig. 45. Windmillgrass *(Chloris verticillata)* plant and spikelet.

Fig. 46. Carolina jointtail (*Coelorachis cylindrica*) inflorescence and spikelet pair.

prairies and along the borders of woods but is infrequently abundant. It occurs mostly in loamy soils.

USE. Carolina jointtail is a native, warm-season perennial that is readily grazed by livestock and wild game but is never abundant enough to be of much significance as forage.

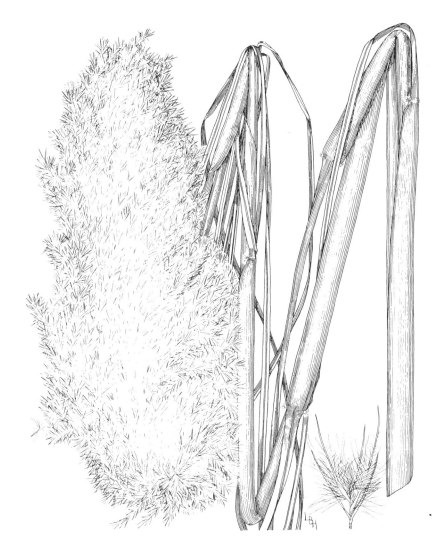

Fig. 47. Pampasgrass *(Cortaderia selloana)* inflorescence and spikelet.

CORTADERIA

47. Pampasgrass *Cortaderia selloana* (Schult.) Aschers. & Graebn.

Stout perennial bunch grass with densely clustered stems and leaves forming a clump as much as 1 m or more in diameter. *Sheaths* broad, rounded, smooth, abruptly narrowing into long, narrow, firm blades mostly 3–10 mm broad and often 1 m or more in length. *Blades* minutely toothed with stout spines on the margins and often on the midnerve. *Ligule* a dense tuft of hairs 3–5 mm long. *Male and female spikelets* on

separate plants, the female spikelets in large, hairy, silvery white panicles, the male spikelets in plain panicles. *Spikelets* with two or three
flowers and with thin, narrow, hairless, single-nerved, pointed glumes.
Lemmas thin, long and narrow, those of the female panicles with long
silky hairs on the back and base and those of the male spikelets hairless.
Plants flowering September to November.

DISTRIBUTION AND HABITAT. Pampasgrass is grown in eastern and
southern Texas as a lawn ornamental and in highway plantings, but this
hardy perennial occasionally persists as a weed of roadsides and waste
areas. It is native to Brazil, Argentina, and Chile.

USE. This grass is of value only as a lawn or roadside ornamental. It
seldom sets seed in Texas and is established by divisions of the clumps.

CYNODON

48. Bermudagrass *Cynodon dactylon* (L.) Pers.

Low, sod-forming perennial forming both stolons and rhizomes, the
rhizomes stout, creeping, and extensive. *Stems* weak, curving upward
from the spreading base, with only the flowering shoots or shoot tips
erect, these 10–50 cm tall. *Sheaths* rounded and hairless except for tufts
of hair on either side of the collar and in the ligular area. *Blades* linear, flat
or folded, hairless, 1–3.5 mm broad, mostly 3–8 cm, but occasionally up
to 14 cm, long. *Inflorescence* of usually two to six slender branches clustered at the stem tip, the branches mostly 2–6 cm long. *Branches* with
numerous awnless spikelets closely placed and overlapping in two rows on
a narrow flattened or triangular branch central axis. *Spikelets* with a single
seed-bearing floret, the spikelet central axis prolonged behind the palea
and often bearing a rudimentary floret. *Glumes* lanceolate, nearly equal,
single-nerved, about two-thirds as long as the lemma. *Lemmas* mostly
2–2.5 mm long, firm, shiny, awnless, acute, laterally compressed and
keeled, three-nerved, the lateral nerves near the margins and the midnerve obscurely hairy. Plants setting seed throughout the year under
favorable growing conditions.

DISTRIBUTION AND HABITAT. Bermudagrass is commonly cultivated
throughout Texas as a lawn and pasture grass, but it is also frequent as a
weed of ditches, vacant lots, and roadways and along streams, lakes, and
marshy swales. Bermudagrass is well adapted to clayey bottomlands that
occasionally are subjected to flooding. It is native to Africa and apparently
was introduced into the United States at an early period, possibly via
Bermuda.

USE. This grass is a warm-season perennial that provides good grazing for livestock and wildlife.

Fig. 48.   Bermudagrass *(Cynodon dactylon)* plant, inflorescence, and spikelet with floret separated from glumes and caryopsis.

DACTYLOCTENIUM

49. Durban crowfootgrass   *Dactyloctenium aegyptium* (L.) Willd.

Tufted or mat-forming annual with weak, usually spreading to erect stems mostly 10–50 cm tall, the stems often rooting at the lower nodes. *Sheaths* laterally compressed and keeled. *Blades* thin, flat or irregularly folded, mostly 2–8 mm broad, usually fringed on the margins with long,

Fig. 49. Durban crowfootgrass (*Dactyloctenium aegyptium*) inflorescence and spikelet.

swollen-based hairs, and often hairy on one or both surfaces. *Inflorescence* with two to six or more thick, radially arranged spikelike branches mostly 1.5–6 cm long. *Branch axis* densely covered with minute hairs near the point of attachment to the main stem, bearing two rows of closely placed, tightly compressed and spreading spikelets from near the base to near the tip, and projecting beyond the terminal spikelet as a sharp point

1–7mm long. *Spikelets* mostly 3–4 mm long, with three to five flowers, breaking up between or above the glumes. *Glumes* firm, hairless, keeled, single-nerved, nearly equal and about as large as the lemma. *First glume* acute or with a minute awn. *Second glume* usually with a short, stout, curved and crooked awn. *Lemmas* similar to the glumes, usually with a short, crooked awn. *Paleas* about as large as the lemmas, with three widely separated nerves. *Grain* plump, reddish brown, 1 mm or slightly less long, rough and ridged. Plants setting seed mostly September to December, but occasionally as early as July.

DISTRIBUTION AND HABITAT. This grass occurs in the eastern two-thirds of the state as a weed of loose, sandy soils often along the shores of lakes and ponds, in intermittent creek beds, and on disturbed soils of cultivated fields. It is an introduced tropical weed.

USE. A casual plant of weedy sites, Durban crowfootgrass has no significance as a forage plant.

DICHANTHELIUM

Key to the species:
Spikelets 2.4 mm or less long
    Hairs of the ligule, at least on the upper leaves, 1.5–6 mm long.....
    .... Woolly dichanthelium, *D. acuminatum*
    Hairs of the ligule less than 1.5 mm long, absent in some species
        Sheaths of the mid-stem leaves hairless on the back; blades dark
        green .... Roundseed dichanthelium, *D. sphaerocarpon*
        Sheaths of the mid-stem leaves (when present) and basal leaves hairy
        on the back; blades yellowish green ....
        .... Openflower dichanthelium, *D. laxiflorum*
Spikelets 2.9–4 mm long .... *D. oligosanthes*

50. Woolly dichanthelium *Dichanthelium acuminatum* (Sw.) Gould & Clark
    Tufted perennial with stems 20–60 cm tall, developing a basal rosette of short leaves in fall, winter, and early spring. *Stem nodes* bearded with soft hairs and with or without a hairless, glandular ring below the node. *Stems* usually branching in age to produce clusters of greatly reduced leafy branchlets, each with a few-flowered inflorescence. *Leaves* hairy, but the blades occasionally nearly hairless. *Sheaths* with closely pressed or spreading hairs on the back as well as on the margins. *Ligule* usually with a band of short hairs below a ring of long hairs (2–6 mm long), the long hairs occasionally present only on the side of the ligule. *Blades of primary stems* lanceolate, mostly 5–12 cm long and 5–12 mm broad. *Panicles* 4–10 cm long, slightly longer than broad, the late-formed inflorescences of the clustered branches with very few flowers. *Spikelets*

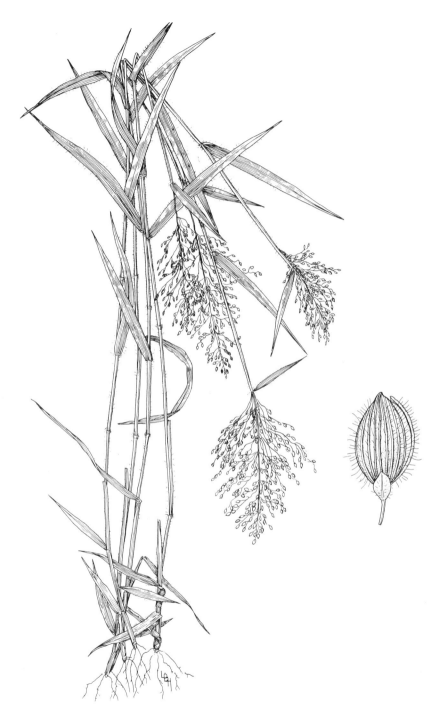

Fig. 50.   Woolly dichanthelium *(Dichanthelium acuminatum)* plant and spikelet.

Fig. 51. Openflower dichanthelium *(Dichanthelium laxiflorum)* plant and two views of spikelet.

downy, narrowly to broadly elliptic, 1.6–2.4 mm long, and mostly on stalks as long as or considerably longer than the spikelet. Plants setting seed mostly April to June and then again in late summer and autumn.

DISTRIBUTION AND HABITAT. Woolly dichanthelium grows in shaded sites in woods or borders of woods, mostly in the eastern portion of the state but occasionally in all regions except the High Plains.

USE. This species is a native, perennial, cool-season, woodland grass that together with the other shade-loving dichantheliums provides a fair amount of forage for livestock and wildlife.

51. Openflower dichanthelium *Dichanthelium laxiflorum* (Lam.) Gould

Plants with a basal tuft of numerous soft, light green blades, these mostly 7–15 cm long and like the blades of the stems. *Stems* slender, hairless on internodes below the panicle, 15–40 cm tall, usually not branching above the base. *Nodes* bearded with soft, spreading hairs. *Sheaths* rather uniformly soft-haired with spreading, often backward-bent hairs 2–3 mm long. *Ligule* a minutely fringed or hairless rim. *Blades* 3–10 mm broad, mostly 7–16 cm long, hairless or inconspicuously hairy on the surfaces, usually fringed with hairs on the margins to well above the middle. *Panicles of primary stems* projecting well above the basal cluster of leaves, mostly 7–12 cm long, typically drooping and few-flowered. *Panicle branches* usually hairy with long, soft hairs. *Late-developed inflorescences* tending to be compact, closely flowered, and usually not elevated above the basal clump of leaves. *Spikelets* broadly ovate or oblong, slightly pointed, 1.7–2.3 mm long. *First glume* thin, 0.5 mm or less long. *Second glume* and lemma of lower floret downy, strongly nerved. Plants setting seed April to June and again in late summer and autumn.

DISTRIBUTION AND HABITAT. This species occurs in the eastern part of the state, mostly in sandy soils of shaded woodland sites.

USE. Openflower dichanthelium is only one of a half-dozen species of that genus that together provide a fair amount of forage in woodland pastures.

52. *Dichanthelium oligosanthes* (Schult.) Gould

Leafy perennial with stems in loose to dense clumps, hairless to densely covered with minute down, mostly 15–85 cm tall. *Stems* much-branched above the base with age. *Sheaths* hairless to densely hairy with stiff hairs, the sheath margins finely to densely fringed with long hairs. *Leaf blades* 3–14 cm long, 3–12 mm broad. *Inflorescence* elevated on a long, slender flower stalk, 4–13 cm long, about half as wide as long. *Late-developed inflorescences* short, projecting little if at all, and with few spikelets. *Spikelets* broadly elliptic to obovate, blunt or pointed, 2.9–4 mm long, 1.2–2.2 mm broad. *Glumes and lower lemma* hairless to soft-

Fig. 52b. Scribner dichanthelium (*Dichanthelium oligosanthes* var. *scribnerianum*) plant (autumn phase), inflorescence (spring phase), and spikelet.

haired, the first glume 0.8–2.2 mm long and narrowly pointed or blunt. Plants setting seed April to June and again in late summer and fall.

Key to the varieties:

Ligule usually 1.6 mm or more long; lower leaf surface usually uniformly woolly, occasionally sparsely soft-haired ....
.... *D. oligosanthes* var. *oligosanthes*
Ligule usually less than 1.6 mm long; lower leaf surface downy to hairless, never woolly ....
..... Scribner dichanthelium, *D. oligosanthes* var. *scribnerianum*

52a. Dichanthelium oligosanthes (Schult.) Gould var. *oligosanthes*
Stems usually soft-downed. *Leaf blades* narrowly pointed, mostly 5–8 mm broad. *Lowermost internode of panicle axis* usually densely softhaired.

DISTRIBUTION AND HABITAT. This variety is found in the eastern twothirds of the state, mostly in shaded, sandy, well-drained but moist sites of woodlands and brushy areas.

USE. Var. *oligosanthes* is also one of the several dichantheliums of shaded woodland habitats that contribute a fair amount of forage for livestock and wildlife.

52b. Scribner dichanthelium *Dichanthelium oligosanthes* (Schult.) Gould var. *scribnerianum* (Nash) Gould
Stems and blades hairless to slightly hairy. *Spikelets* 2.9–3.8 mm long and mostly 1.4–1.8 mm broad, hairless to soft-haired. *Lowermost internode of panicle axis* hairless, rough, or moderately hairy.

DISTRIBUTION AND HABITAT. Scribner dichanthelium is reported from all regions of the state and usually grows on loamy-clay sites in open or brushy areas.

USE. This variety is a native, cool-season perennial that provides fair forage grass for livestock and wildlife, producing a moderate amount of green grass during the winter and early spring months and also developing herbage following summer rains.

53. Roundseed dichanthelium *Dichanthelium sphaerocarpon* (Ell.) Gould
Tufted perennial, producing a rosette of basal leaves during the winter and early spring and then developing stems 20–80 cm tall. *Stems* sparingly branched at upper nodes in age. *Leaves of basal rosette* broad and short, usually with wavy whitish margins. *Sheaths* usually downy with fine, soft hairs on one or both margins, otherwise hairless. *Blades* thick, hairless on the surfaces, edged with a few widely spaced, stout, swollenbased hairs on the lower margins, rounded at their base. *Panicles* open, many-flowered, 6–15 cm long, slightly narrower than long, with hairless

Fig. 53. Roundseed dichanthelium *(Dichanthelium sphaerocarpon)* plant and spikelet.

main axis and branches. *Spikelets* downy to hairless, 1.4–2 mm long, broadly oblong or obovoid to nearly round at maturity. Plants setting seed late March to June and again in late summer and autumn.

DISTRIBUTION AND HABITAT. Roundseed dichanthelium occurs throughout the state except in the High Plains and Rolling Plains. It is usually found in shaded woodland sites.

USE. Together with the other woodland dichantheliums, this native, perennial, cool-season grass provides fair forage for livestock and wildlife.

DICHANTHIUM

54. Kleberg bluestem   *Dichanthium annulatum* Stapf *(Andropogon annulatus* Forsk.*)*

Strong perennial, usually developing long, stout, creeping rhizomes. *Nodes* of stems and rhizomes bearded with long, soft hairs. *Sheaths* hairless, usually much shorter than the internodes. *Blades* long and linear, mostly 6–25 cm long and 3–6 mm broad, hairless or hairy with stiff, swollen-based hairs. *Inflorescence* of three to five (occasionally one to eight) slender unbranched branches clustered at the stem tip, these mostly 4–7 cm long. *Main axis of inflorescence and stalk just below inflorescence* hairless. *Spikelets* greenish to purple-tinged, 4–5 mm long, in pairs of one stalkless and awned and one stalked and awnless. *Stalkless (awned) spikelets* seed-bearing. *Awns* brownish, twisted and twice-bent, 1.5–2.5 cm long. Plants setting seed throughout the year under favorable growing conditions.

DISTRIBUTION AND HABITAT. Kleberg bluestem was introduced as a pasture grass and is now sparingly established on rangelands, along roadsides, in ditches, and on vacant city lots in southern Texas and along the Gulf Coast.

USE. This coarse, rather stemmy warm-season forage grass is native to China, India, and Africa. Kleberg bluestem provides fair grazing for cattle and horses.

DIGITARIA

Key to the species:
Plants perennial; axis of the inflorescence branch not winged . . . .
. . . . California cottontop, *D. californica*
Plants annual; axis of the inflorescence branch broadly winged . . . .
. . . . Southern crabgrass, *D. ciliaris*

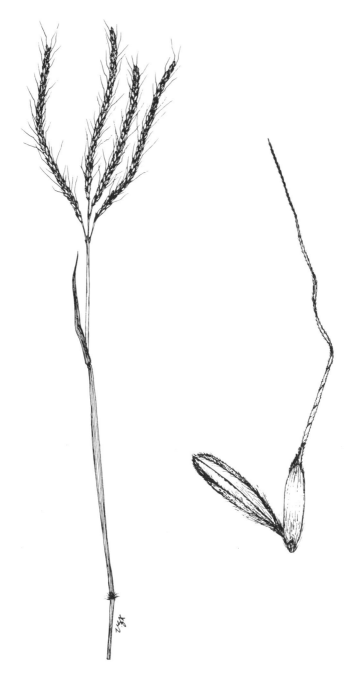

Fig. 54.   Kleberg bluestem (*Dichanthium annulatum*) inflorescence and spikelet pair.

Fig. 55. California cottontop *(Digitaria californica)* plant, inflorescence, and spikelet.

55. California cottontop *Digitaria californica* (Benth.) Henr.

Tufted, leafy perennial with stiffly erect stems mostly 50–100 cm tall, developed from a firm, knotty base covered with densely downy scale leaves. *Leaves* hairless, except for the felty-downy lower sheaths, or sparsely haired. *Blades* mostly 2–6 mm broad. *Panicles* narrow, densely flowered, usually 8–12 cm long, typically with closely appressed, mostly unbranched primary branches. *Spikelets* narrow, pointed, hairy, 3–4 mm long. *Second glume and margins of lemma of lower floret* densely hairy with silvery or purple-tinged hairs 2–4 mm long. *Lemma of lower floret* hairless on back. *Lemma of upper (seed-bearing) floret* ovate to lanceolate, abruptly narrowing to a short awn. Plants setting seed July to November.

DISTRIBUTION AND HABITAT. California cottontop may be found throughout most of Texas, except the Post Oak Savanna and Pineywoods of eastern Texas, on open, well-drained soils.

USE. This native, warm-season perennial grows on a wide variety of soil types and provides good grazing for livestock and fair grazing for wildlife. It is palatable throughout the year and is frequently overgrazed, but it responds well to periodic deferment from grazing.

56. Southern crabgrass *Digitaria ciliaris* (Retz.) Koel.

Annual with weak upward-bent or spreading stems, these branching at the base and rooting at the lower nodes. *Sheaths* downy with swollen-based hairs. *Blades* 5–10 mm broad, usually hairy on both surfaces with swollen-based hairs. *Inflorescence* with usually four to nine unbranched branches 6–14 cm long, these radially arranged at the stem tip or at the tip and in one or two whorls below. *Axis of inflorescence branch* strongly three-sided and slightly winged, with spikelets in unequally stalked pairs, the members of a pair essentially similar. *Spikelets* 2.8–3.5 mm long. *First glume* minute, scalelike. *Second glume* 1.6–2.7 mm long, downy on the margins. *Lemma of lower floret* with five unequally spaced strong nerves. *Lemma of upper floret* firm, light brown, pointed, about as long as the spikelet. Plants setting seed June to November.

DISTRIBUTION AND HABITAT. Southern crabgrass is frequent throughout the state as a common weed of rangeland in poor condition, roadsides, lawns, field borders, and gardens.

USE. This species is a common annual, cool-season grass of disturbed soils, presumably introduced and of no economic value.

Fig. 56. Southern crabgrass *(Digitaria ciliaris)* plant, spikelet pair, and opposite side of spikelet.

DISTICHLIS

57. Saltgrass   *Distichlis spicata* (L.) Greene

Tufted or sod-forming perennial with stems 10–60 cm tall from stout, creeping rhizomes and with several to many nodes and short internodes. Leaves firm, thick, short, overlapping, double-ranked and in regular rows, the lower leaves reduced and scalelike. *Sheaths* rounded on the back, hairless or with minute down. *Blades* mostly 2–10 cm long and 1–4 mm broad, inrolled when dried. *Inflorescence* a contracted panicle or spikelike raceme 2.5–8 cm long with large, several-flowered, awnless spikelets on short, stout branches and stalks. *Male and female spikelets* in separate but similar inflorescences, the female panicles with spikelets more congested and irregularly spreading than those of the male panicles. *Spikelets* 6–20 mm long, laterally flattened, mostly with five to fifteen flowers, breaking up above the glumes and between florets. *Glumes* slightly unequal, thick and firm, hairless, pointed, with three to nine nerves, the lateral nerves often indistinct. *Lemmas* similar to the glumes but longer and broader, with five to eleven nerves, laterally compressed and keeled, mostly 3–6 mm long, acute and often boat-shaped at the tip. *Paleas* about as long as the lemmas, the two nerves keeled and slightly to strongly winged. At maturity the paleas of the female florets bowed out at their base. Plants setting seed throughout the year under favorable growing conditions.

Key to the varieties:

Stems 10–60 cm tall; leaf blades not over 15 cm long; female (pistillate) inflorescences, and usually the male (staminate) ones, congested, the short stalks not readily visible; female spikelets with five to nine flowers; male spikelets with five to twenty flowers; plants of coastal areas .... Coastal saltgrass, *D. spicata* var. *spicata*
Stems 10–35 cm tall; leaf blades up to 20 cm long; female and male spikelets with five to twenty flowers; inland plants ....
.... Inland saltgrass, *D. spicata* var. *stricta*

57a. Coastal saltgrass   *Distichlis spicata* (L.) Greene var. *spicata*

DISTRIBUTION AND HABITAT. As its name implies, coastal saltgrass occurs along the coast in saline marshes and low moist or swampy pastureland. It often forms extensive colonies.

USE. Coastal saltgrass makes most of its growth during the summer, but it has the most value for forage in the winter. This grass is grazed by cattle and horses. Regrowth following controlled burning in the fall provides good feed for wild ducks and geese.

Fig. 57a. Coastal saltgrass *(Distichlis spicata* var. *spicata)* plant and separate inflorescence.

102 : Common Texas Grasses

57b. Inland saltgrass *Distichlis spicata* (L.) Greene var. *stricta* (Torr.) Beetle

DISTRIBUTION AND HABITAT. Inland saltgrass is occasional throughout central, northwestern, and western Texas. In a few moist or wet alkaline or saline areas it is locally abundant.

USE. This native, perennial, warm-season grass provides fair forage for livestock and poor forage for wildlife. It is grazed by horses and cattle during the summer when it is green and during other seasons when it is the only forage available.

ECHINOCHLOA

Key to the species:

Primary inflorescence branches unbranched, usually 2 cm or less long; spikelets awnless, arranged in four regular rows on the branch axis; palea of the lower floret well developed, at least half as long as the lemma; hairs of panicle branches short or long, not swollen-based . . .
. . . . Junglerice, *E. colona*

Primary inflorescence branches often rebranched, at least some branches usually more than 2 cm long; spikelets in regular rows or not; palea of the lower floret present or absent

Palea of the lower floret absent or nearly so; spikelets awnless or with awns 1 cm or less long; stiff, swollen-based hairs on the inflorescence branches absent or shorter than the spikelets . . . . .
. . . . Alkali barnyardgrass, *E. crus-pavonis* var. *macera*

Palea of the lower floret present, more than half as long as the lower lemma; spikelets awnless or with awns 2–5 cm long; stiff, swollen-based hairs longer than the spikelets present on the inflorescence branches . . . . Common barnyardgrass, *E. crusgalli* var. *crusgalli*

58. Junglerice *Echinochloa colona* (L.) Link

Annual with slender, weak, spreading, freely branching stems 10–70 cm long. *Leaves* hairless, without ligules, the blades thin and flat, usually 3–7 mm broad. In one form, called "zonale," the blades with purple bars, V's, or blotches. *Inflorescence* short, few-flowered, usually with three to seven unbranched primary branches, these mostly 1–2 cm long. *Nodes of main inflorescence axis and branches* hairless or with a few short to moderately long hairs, these never swollen-based. *Spikelets* 2.5–3 mm long, awnless, usually inconspicuously hairy with fine, short hairs, these never swollen-based. *Palea of lower floret* well developed. *Lemma of upper floret* elliptic, usually 2.6–2.9 mm long, the firm portion rounded at the apex. Plants setting seed mostly in summer and fall.

Fig. 58.   Junglerice *(Echinochloa colona)* plant and spikelet.

104 : Common Texas Grasses

DISTRIBUTION AND HABITAT. An introduced weed that is present throughout the state and thrives in disturbed soils, junglerice is most frequent in gardens, moist ditches, weedy fields, and waste places. It is widespread in tropical and subtropical regions of both hemispheres.

USE. Junglerice is a relatively "inoffensive" warm-season weedy annual. This grass has essentially no forage value, but along with the other species of *Echinochloa* it provides a considerable amount of birdseed.

59. **Common barnyardgrass** *Echinochloa crusgalli* (L.) Beauv. var. *crusgalli*
Leafy annual, with stiffly erect or spreading and upward-curving stems mostly 30–100 cm tall, but occasionally twice that tall. *Stems* hairless, many-noded, the nodes slightly swollen. *Sheaths* hairless. *Blades* mostly 0.5–2.5 cm broad and as much as 40 cm long, rough or sparsely hairy, the margins finely toothed. *Panicles* mostly 10–25 cm long, with usually five to twenty-five closely appressed or spreading branches, the longer branches rebranched. *Spikelets* mostly 2.8–4 mm long and 1.1–2.3 mm broad, ovate or elliptic, awned or awnless, variously rough or hairy to nearly hairless. *Lower floret* neuter, the lemma awnless or with an awn to more than 5 cm long, the palea large, well developed. *Lemma of upper floret* firm, shiny, pointed, with a sharply differentiated, withering membranous tip. *Anthers* 0.5–1 mm long. *Grain* ovate or elliptic, 1.3–2.2 mm long and 1–1.8 mm broad. Plants setting seed July to November.

DISTRIBUTION AND HABITAT. Common barnyardgrass grows throughout the state in small or large colonies, mainly in ditches, in wet meadows, and along marshes and lakes.

USE. This grass is a warm-season, introduced, weedy annual of little value for livestock or wildlife forage, but its grain crop provides considerable food for wild ducks, geese, and other birds.

60. **Alkali barnyardgrass** *Echinochloa crus-pavonis* (H.B.K.) Schult. var. *macera* (Wiegand) Gould
Tufted, relatively hairless annual, with usually several-noded stems 60–100 cm tall. *Leaves* with flat, shiny, elongate blades mostly 7–15 mm broad. *Panicles* usually 10–20 cm long, with short, stiffly erect branches on a relatively stout central axis. *Spikelets* 2.8–3.1 mm long, awnless or minutely awned, the lemma of the lower floret occasionally with a short awn. *Palea of lower floret* absent or minute. *Lemma of upper floret* firm, grayish, narrowly elliptic, with a well-differentiated, membranous, withering tip. Plants setting seed mostly May to November.

DISTRIBUTION AND HABITAT. Alkali barnyardgrass occurs throughout the state, except in the Pineywoods, in ditches, on field borders, and in vacant city lots and waste places. It is probably the most prevalent barnyardgrass in the state.

Fig. 59. Common barnyardgrass (*Echinochloa crusgalli* var. *crusgalli*) inflorescence and spikelet.

Fig. 60.   Alkali barnyardgrass (*Echinochloa crus-pavonis* var. *macera*) plant and two views of spikelet.

USE. This species is a warm-season, introduced annual of low forage value for livestock and large game animals. Its grain, like that of common barnyardgrass, provides considerable food for wild ducks, geese, and other birds.

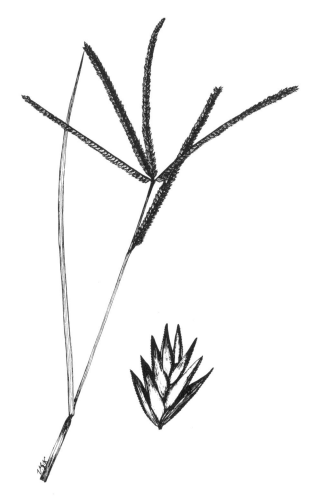

Fig. 61.   Goosegrass *(Eleusine indica)* inflorescence and spikelet.

ELEUSINE

61. Goosegrass   *Eleusine indica* (L.) Gaertn.

Succulent, leafy annual. *Stems* erect or spreading, occasionally forming stolons at the base, mostly 15–70 cm long but much shorter on
mowed, grazed, or otherwise disturbed plants. *Sheaths* compressed laterally and strongly keeled, hairless or sparsely long-haired on the margins. *Blades* elongate, linear, mostly 3–8 mm broad, flat or folded and
keeled at their base, hairless or with long hairs along the margins and
sometimes on the upper surface near the ligule. *Inflorescence* with two,
occasionally one to eight, spikelike branches, these mostly radiating from

the stem tip but frequently with one or two branches present well below the tip whorl. *Inflorescence branches* 3–15 cm long, with a flattened, winged axis bearing closely overlapping, awnless spikelets in two rows. *Spikelets* 3–6 mm long, with three to six flowers. *Glumes* pointed, hairless, the first single-nerved and the second larger, with three to seven nerves. *Lemmas* hairless, somewhat laterally compressed and keeled, acute or rounded at the tip. *Grains* 1–2 mm long, plump, cross-ridged and rough, the seed loosely enclosed by a thin fruit coat. Plants setting seed mostly in late summer and autumn, occasionally flowering in late spring.

DISTRIBUTION AND HABITAT. Goosegrass occurs throughout the state as a weed of lawns, gardens, ditches, and other areas of disturbed soils.

USE. This grass is an introduced annual of no value as a forage plant.

ELYMUS

Key to the species:

Glumes not bowed out or only slightly bowed out at their base, flat and only slightly thickened at their base; lemma awns 1.5–5 cm long .... Canada wildrye, *E. canadensis*
Glumes strongly bowed out at their base, hard, thickened, and shiny at their base; lemma awns usually 0.5–2.5 cm long ....
.... Virginia wildrye, *E. virginicus*

62. Canada wildrye *Elymus canadensis* L.

Tufted perennial with stems 80–150 cm tall in small or occasionally large clumps. *Leaf auricles* slender and fragile, usually developed on either side of the junction of sheath and blade. *Blades* flat or folded, elongate, mostly 4–12 mm broad, hairless or hairy. *Inflorescence* an erect or nodding spike 8–20 cm long, the spikelets paired or in threes at each node. *Spikelets* mostly with three to five flowers. *Glumes* about equal, tapering to an awn usually longer than the body. *Lemmas* hairless, bristly or rough, mostly 0.8–1 cm or more long, with wavy awns 1.5–5 cm long, these usually curving outward at maturity. Plants setting seed March to June, infrequently in summer and early autumn.

DISTRIBUTION AND HABITAT. Canada wildrye is found throughout Texas except in the southern portion of South Texas. It grows mostly in shaded sites, frequently along fence rows and borders of woods, and in moist canyons and ravines.

USE. This species is a native, cool-season perennial that provides good grazing for livestock and fair grazing for wildlife.

Fig. 62.   Canada wildrye *(Elymus canadensis)* plant and spikelet with glumes separated from floret.

63. Virginia wildrye   *Elymus virginicus* L.

Perennial with stems in small clusters, mostly 60–120 cm tall. *Leaves* hairless or the blades minutely hairy. *Blades* long, mostly 5–15 mm broad. *Inflorescence* a stiffly erect, bristly spike mostly 8–15 cm long but occasionally much longer, often partly enclosed by the upper sheath.

Fig. 63. Virginia wildrye *(Elymus virginicus)* inflorescence.

Spikelets mostly with three to five flowers. *Glumes* yellowish, hard, strongly nerved above but nerveless and bowed out at the base, the tip often somewhat curved, tapering into a straight awn shorter or longer than the body. *Lemma* hairless or sparsely hairy, with a straight or slightly curved awn 0.5–2.5 cm long. Plants setting seed April to June, occasionally as late as September.

DISTRIBUTION AND HABITAT. Virginia wildrye is occasional in all regions of Texas except the Panhandle and the western mountains and is most abundant in the eastern half of the state. It is a grass of shaded banks, fence rows, and open woodlands.

USE. This grass is a native, cool-season perennial that provides good grazing for both livestock and wildlife along shaded ravines, wooded canyons, and moist, open bottoms.

ELYONURUS

64. Pan American balsamscale *Elyonurus tripsacoides* Humb. & Bonpl. *ex* Willd.

Tufted perennial with stems mostly 60–120 cm tall, in small clusters from knotty bases, often forming rhizomes, branching at the upper nodes to produce stiffly erect spikelike inflorescences. *Stem nodes* hairless. *Leaves* essentially hairless, but with a few swollen-based hairs in the vicinity of the ligule and often on the upper portion of the sheath. *Blades* long, threadlike, flat or more commonly inrolled, mostly only 1–2 mm broad, the basal ones 16–30 cm or more long. *Inflorescence* a spikelike raceme 6–15 cm long with a stout, flattened central axis that is hairy on the margins. *Spikelet stalks* similar to the central axis joints, thick, broad and flattened, hairy on the back, at least on the lower half, slightly shorter than the stalked spikelets. *Spikelets* awnless, in pairs of one nearly stalkless and seed-bearing and one stalked with stamens only, the longer-stalked spikelet similar in size and appearance to the short-stalked one. *Short-stalked spikelets* mostly 6–8 mm long, and the longer-stalked spikelets slightly shorter. *First glume of short-stalked spikelet* firm, broadly rounded, usually hairless on the back below the tip, hairy on the margins, irregularly lobed or cleft, and with stiff hairs at the tip. *Lemma of short-stalked spikelet* thin and membranous, the palea absent. Plants setting seed May to November.

DISTRIBUTION AND HABITAT. Pan American balsamscale occurs along the coast and in southern Texas on sandy soils of coastal grasslands and woods openings.

A second species of *Elyonurus* is present in far western Texas. This species, with stems downy below the nodes and with densely woolly glumes, is *E. barbiculmis* Hack., commonly known as woolspike balsamscale.

USE. This native perennial is seldom sufficiently abundant to provide significant amounts of forage for livestock or wildlife.

ENNEAPOGON

65. Feather pappusgrass *Enneapogon desvauxii* Beauv.

Low, tufted perennial with narrow, spikelike panicles. *Stems* 10–50 cm tall, usually hairy at least on the nodes. *Sheaths* rounded on the back, usually hairy, much shorter than the stem internodes. *Blades* slender and threadlike, hairy at least on the upper surface, 0.5–2 mm broad and mostly 2–12 cm long, inrolled or folded when dried. *Panicles* densely contracted, 2–9 cm long and 6–12 mm thick, grayish or lead-colored. *Spikelets* mostly 5–7 cm long, including the awns, and usually three-flowered, with only the lower floret seed-bearing. *Glumes* nearly equal,

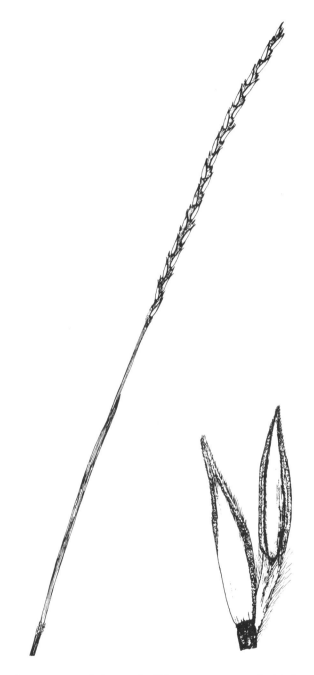

Fig. 64.   Pan American balsamscale *(Elyonurus tripsacoides)* inflorescence and
spikelet pair.

Fig. 65. Feather pappusgrass *(Enneapogon desvauxii)* plant, spikelet with glumes (above), and spikelet without glumes (below).

but the first usually broader, thin and membranous, hairy, the first 3–5 mm long, with five to seven nerves, and the second similar but with only three or four nerves in some spikelets. *Lemmas* downy, broad, much shorter than the glumes, firm, rounded on the back, the body mostly 1.5–2 mm long, with nine strong nerves and nine equal, feathery awns mostly 3–4 mm long. *Palea* about as long as the body of the lemma, with widely spreading nerves. Plants setting seed July to November, but occasionally earlier.

DISTRIBUTION AND HABITAT. Feather pappusgrass grows in the central and western regions of the state and is frequent on dry, open slopes.

USE. This grass is a warm-season, native perennial adapted to dry open or brushy habitats. Feather pappusgrass develops little herbage and is not significant as a forage grass.

ERAGROSTIS

Key to the species:

Plants annual; glumes and lemmas usually with glandular pits in the
keels . . . . Stinkgrass, *E. cilianensis*

Plants perennial; glumes without glandular pits in the keels

Spikelets with short or long stalks; if the stalks all short, then the
branches not long but stiffly spreading and unbranched above
the base

Lateral spikelet stalks infrequently as much as 1 mm long . . . .
. . . . Red lovegrass, *E. secundiflora*

Lateral spikelet stalks mostly 1–6 mm or more long

Second glume or lemmas usually 2.4–3 mm or more long

Spikelets lead-colored, mostly or all on appressed stalks 0.5 mm
or less long . . . . Weeping lovegrass, *E. curvula*

Spikelets light brown or purplish on long, often spreading stalks
12 mm or more long . . . . Sand lovegrass, *E. trichodes*

Second glume and lemmas usually 1.4–2.2 mm long . . . .
. . . . Plains lovegrass *E. intermedia*

Spikelets stalkless; panicle branches long, stiffly spreading, without
secondary branching except for spurlike branches at the bases of
the lower branches . . . . Tumble lovegrass, *E. sessilispica*

66. Stinkgrass *Eragrostis cilianensis* (All.) E. Mosher

Tufted annual with weak, spreading stems 10–60 cm tall, usually
with glandular tissue below the nodes. *Sheaths* hairless except for soft,
straight hairs at the throat. *Blades* hairless, flat, lanceolate, sometimes
folded, with glandular pits in the midrib on the lower surface, 10–20 cm
long, 2.5–7 mm wide. *Panicles* ovate to oblong, densely flowered to open,
5.5–16 cm long. *Spikelets* large, short-stalked, slightly compressed laterally, 6–20 mm long and 2–4 mm wide, with twelve to forty flowers.
Glumes keeled, with minute glandular pits on the keels. *Lemmas* 2.2–2.8
mm long, dull grayish green, with three conspicuous nerves, usually with
glandular pits on the keels. *Grains* 0.5–0.8 mm long. Plants setting seed
mostly August through October.

DISTRIBUTION AND HABITAT. Stinkgrass is found throughout the state in
ditches and waste places, mostly as a weed of disturbed soil.

USE. This grass is an introduced, warm-season weed of no forage
significance.

67. Weeping lovegrass *Eragrostis curvula* (Schrad.) Nees

Stout perennial bunch grass with tough stems in large clumps,
mostly 75–150 cm tall. *Sheaths* shorter than the stem internodes, the
basal ones densely soft-haired on the back near the base and less so on the
margins, the upper sheaths nearly hairless but with long, soft hairs at the

Fig. 66. Stinkgrass (*Eragrostis cilianensis*) inflorescence and spikelet.

throat. *Blades* long and threadlike, those of the stem leaves 20–30 cm long, and 1–1.4 mm wide, the basal leaf blades much longer and arching towards the ground. *Panicles* open, oblong to ovate, 25–40 cm long, 8–12 cm wide. *Panicle branches* slender, ascending to spreading, mostly 5–7 cm long. *Spikelets* somewhat closely bunched on short stalks, linear-lanceolate, laterally compressed, 6–10 mm long, 1.4–1.6 mm wide, with six to twelve flowers, breaking up along the axis. *Glumes* membranous, ovate, sharp-pointed, the first about 1.8 mm long, and the second about 2.8 mm long. *Florets* closely placed. *Lemmas* membranous, overlapping, grayish green, ovate, sharp-pointed, 2.2–2.6 mm long and about 1.4 mm wide, with the lateral nerves conspicuous. *Paleas* translucent, rough on the keels. *Grains* ellipsoidal, about 1.4 mm long. Plants setting seed in late spring, summer, and fall.

DISTRIBUTION AND HABITAT. Weeping lovegrass is planted as a forage grass throughout the state and is persistent on roadsides and in sandy fields and waste areas. It is a native of South Africa introduced into the southern United States.

USE. A vigorous warm-season bunch grass that has been introduced in many localities as a forage grass, weeping lovegrass provides fair grazing for livestock but relatively poor grazing for wildlife.

116 : Common Texas Grasses

Fig. 67.   Weeping lovegrass (*Eragrostis curvula*) plant and spikelet.

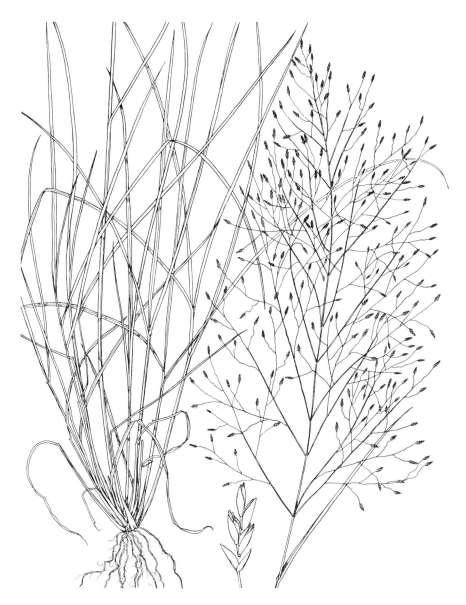

Fig. 68. Plains lovegrass (*Eragrostis intermedia*) plant and spikelet.

68. Plains lovegrass *Eragrostis intermedia* Hitchc.

Perennial bunch grass with stems 55–90 cm tall. *Sheaths* hairless except for tufts of hairs on the throat and the upper margins. *Blades* narrow, usually flat, mostly 15–25 cm long and 2–3 mm wide. *Panicles* open, ovate, 20–40 cm long and 15–30 cm wide. *Panicle branches* ascending to spreading, 10–25 cm long, with small, awnless spikelets on long, slender stalks. *Spikelets* ovate, 4–7 mm long, 1.6–1.8 mm wide, with five to eleven flowers, the central axis usually not breaking up. *Glumes* thin, pointed, the first 1.2–1.8 mm long and the second 1.4–2 mm long. *Lemmas* firm, pointed, grayish green to reddish purple, 1.8–2.2 mm long, about 1.2 mm wide, with three inconspicuous nerves. *Grains* oblong, about 0.8 mm long. Plants setting seed June through November.

DISTRIBUTION AND HABITAT. Plains lovegrass grows throughout the state, except in the easternmost portion, on sandy, clayey, and rocky ground, often in disturbed soil.

USE. A native, warm-season perennial providing good grazing for livestock and poor grazing for wildlife, plains lovegrass usually grows with other perennial grasses in mixed grassland associations.

69. **Red lovegrass**   *Eragrostis secundiflora* Presl. (*Eragrostis oxylepis* [Torr.] Torr.)

Tufted perennial with stems 30–75 cm tall. *Sheaths* hairy at the throat and sometimes downy on the margins. *Blades* flat to inrolled, usually 10–15 cm long and 2–2.5 mm wide, with long hairs above the ligule. *Panicles* usually narrow and contracted, the lower branches occasionally spreading, 5–30 cm long, 1–15 cm wide. *Spikelets* short-stalked and densely clustered, awnless, strongly compressed laterally, 6–20 mm long, 3–5 mm wide, with ten to twenty-four flowers. *Glumes* tapering to a point, the first 2.5–3 mm long, and the second 3–4 mm long. *Lemmas* closely overlapped, broadly ovate, usually abruptly pointed, straw-colored to reddish purple, 1.6–2.4 mm long, with the three nerves conspicuous. *Grains* ellipsoidal, about 1 mm long. Plants setting seed May through June, and often again August through December.

DISTRIBUTION AND HABITAT. Red lovegrass occurs in the northern, northeastern, and central portions of the state in both sandy and clayey soils. It is often somewhat weedy.

USE. This species is a native, warm-season perennial of poor grazing value for both livestock and wildlife and seldom sufficiently abundant to be of significance as a forage grass.

70. **Tumble lovegrass**   *Eragrostis sessilispica* Buckl.

Tufted perennial with somewhat wiry stems 30–90 cm tall. *Sheaths* overlapping below, hairy at the throat. *Blades* flat or inrolled, usually hairless, 10–30 cm long, 1–3 mm wide. *Panicles* open, with relatively few strong, stiffly spreading branches 25–65 cm long and 10–25 cm wide, the panicle finally breaking off and becoming a tumbleweed. *Panicle branches* distant, few-flowered, unbranched except for a few spur branches near their bases, often 8–25 cm long. *Spikelets* stalkless, widely spaced, 5–12.5 mm long and 2–3 mm wide, with five to twelve flowers. *Glumes* firm, persistent, tapering to a point, the first 2–6 mm long, and the second

Fig. 69.   Red lovegrass *(Eragrostis secundiflora)* inflorescence and spikelet.

3–6 mm long. *Lemmas* firm, loosely overlapping, straw-colored to purple-tinged, narrowly pointed, 3–5 mm long, 2–4 mm wide, conspicuously three-nerved. *Paleas* firm, bowed out, fringed on the keels. *Grain* ellipsoidal, tapering to the tip, about 1.2 mm long. Plants setting seed April through September.

DISTRIBUTION AND HABITAT. Tumble lovegrass is found in sandy prairies from central Oklahoma southward through the central portion of Texas, but not in extreme eastern or western Texas.

USE. This species is a native, warm-season perennial of poor grazing value for both livestock and wildlife.

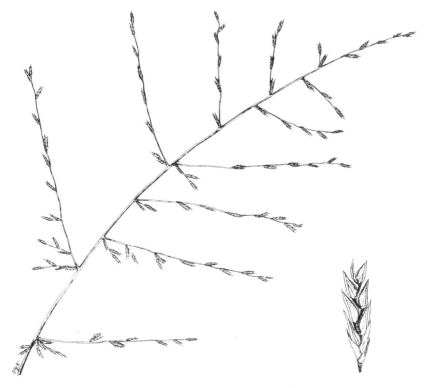

Fig. 70. Tumble lovegrass (*Eragrostis sessilispica*) inflorescence and spikelet.

71. Sand lovegrass *Eragrostis trichodes* (Nutt.) Wood
  Slender, tufted perennial with stiffly erect stems 60–160 cm tall.
Sheaths with a tuft of hairs on either side at the tip, occasionally hairy on
the back or margins. *Blades* flat, long and narrow, gradually tapering to a
point, mostly 15–40 cm long and 1–8 mm broad, hairless except for a few
hairs above the ligule. *Panicles* large, open, long, usually 35–55 cm long
and 7–30 cm wide, with ascending or spreading branches. *Spikelets* awnless, with four to eighteen flowers, extremely variable in length but
mostly 4–10 mm long, at least some of the spikelets on long, flexuous
stalks. *Glumes* thin, pointed, the first 1.8–4 mm long, and the second
1.8–3.4 mm long. *Lemmas* three-nerved, 2.4–3.4 mm long, at first
straw-colored, but maturing brownish or purplish. *Grains* cylindrical,
about 1 mm long. Plants setting seed July to December.
  DISTRIBUTION AND HABITAT. Sand lovegrass is widespread in the northern and central portions of the state, mostly in deep sand and in woodlands and along borders of woods.
  USE. This native perennial bunch grass provides good grazing for
livestock and poor grazing for wildlife. Although sand lovegrass is highly

Fig. 71. Sand lovegrass (*Eragrostis trichodes*) plant.

palatable to livestock, it is seldom present in large stands. It cures well and provides good fall and winter grazing.

Fig. 72.   Sugarcane plumegrass *(Erianthus giganteus)* plant and spikelet.

ERIANTHUS

72. Sugarcane plumegrass *Erianthus giganteus* (Walt.) Muhl.

Stout perennial with stems 1.3–3 m tall, densely clumped from a hard, knotty base. *Nodes* densely bearded with hairs 2–6 mm long, at least some hairs usually persistent with age. *Sheaths* stiffly hairy at least near the tip, losing the hairs with age. *Ligule and collar region of leaf* densely soft-haired. *Blades* mostly 0.8–20 mm broad and 90 cm or more long, with short hairs closely appressed against one or both surfaces. *Panicle* large, dense, and many-flowered, mostly 15–50 cm long and as much as 8 cm thick, conspicuously hairy. *Panicle branches* readily breaking up at the joints when mature. *Axis of panicle and stem internode below panicle* soft-haired with closely appressed or slightly spreading hairs. *Hairs of spikelet base* dense, brownish. *Spikelets* all alike and seed-bearing, mostly in pairs of one stalkless and one stalked, but with one stalkless and two stalked at the branch tips. Spikelets brownish, mostly 6–8 mm long. *Awn of lemma* straight or slightly curved, cylindrical and untwisted, 12–25 mm long. Plants setting seed September to November.

DISTRIBUTION AND HABITAT. Sugarcane plumegrass occurs in the eastern third of the state, mostly in partial shade in wet soils of bogs, swales, or swamps, and often in marshy roadside ditches.

USE. This species is of little or no importance as a forage grass.

ERIOCHLOA

73. Texas cupgrass *Eriochloa sericea* (Scheele) Munro

Perennial bunch grass with stems 50–100 cm tall, strictly erect from a firm base that does not form rhizomes. *Stem nodes* downy. *Sheaths*, at least the lower ones, finely hairy. *Blades* elongate, mostly 2–3 mm broad, flat or more frequently inrolled, hairless or finely haired. *Inflorescence* slender, contracted, and elongated, usually of four to ten short, widely spaced, and strictly erect branches 1.5–3 cm long. *Inflorescence axis and branches* softly hairy, with at least some hairs 2–4 mm long. *Spikelets* ovate, with closely appressed hairs, awnless, 3.6–4.2 mm long. *First glume* reduced and fused with the spikelet base to form a cup or disk. *Second glume and lower lemma* about equal, tapering to a narrow tip, longer than the upper floret (grain). *Lemma of upper floret* firm or hard, finely roughened, with a minute awn tip. Plants setting seed April (occasionally March) to November.

DISTRIBUTION AND HABITAT. Texas cupgrass grows throughout the central and southern portions of the state in prairies and grassy openings in scrub woodlands.

USE. This species is a highly palatable forage plant that survives only under moderate grazing pressure and persists on the more heavily grazed

Fig. 73.   Texas cupgrass *(Eriochloa sericea)* plant, spikelet, and floret.

pastures only in the protection of shrubs. It is a native, warm-season perennial that provides good grazing for livestock and poor grazing for wildlife.

Fig. 74. Hairy tridens *(Erioneuron pilosum)* plant and spikelet.

126 : Common Texas Grasses

ERIONEURON

Key to the species:

Spikelets in leafy clusters, the inflorescences not surpassing or scarcely surpassing the stiff, spine-tipped leaf blades; plants often with slender, wiry stolons .... Fluffgrass, *E. pulchellum*

Spikelets on an elongated, leafless floral axis; plants rarely forming stolons .... Hairy tridens, *E. pilosum*

74. Hairy tridens   *Erioneuron pilosum* (Buckl.) Nash.

Low, tufted perennial without creeping or looping stolons. *Stems* mostly 10–30 cm tall, usually with only one node elevated above the basal cluster of leaves. *Lower sheaths* laterally compressed and keeled. *Blades* thick, narrow, flat, hairless, mostly 2–8 cm long and 1–2 mm broad, with thick whitish margins, and abruptly pointed but not spiny at the tip. *Inflorescence* a contracted panicle or raceme 2–3 cm (rarely up to 4 cm) long and 1.5–2 cm broad, with usually four to ten large, pale spikelets. *Spikelets* mostly 10–16 mm long and with seven to eighteen closely overlapping florets. *Glumes* gradually narrowing to the tip, 4.5–6 mm long. *Lower lemmas* about as long as the glumes, strongly three-nerved, densely fringed with down, with long, silvery hairs on the nerves and also on the margins and between nerves near the base, and with a rounded or minutely notched apex and an awn 1–2 mm long. *Grain* 1.3–1.5 mm long. Plants setting seed mostly April to July, but occasionally to October.

DISTRIBUTION AND HABITAT. Found throughout the state except in the far eastern portion, mostly on open rangelands and pastures, hairy tridens is frequent along road rights-of-way, usually in limey soils.

USE. Hairy tridens is a relatively poor forage plant for livestock and wildlife. It has some value in retarding soil erosion in dry regions subject to occasional heavy rains.

75. Fluffgrass   *Erioneuron pulchellum* (H.B.K.) Tateoka

Low, tufted perennial often developing slender, wiry, looping stolons. Plants often appearing annual. *Stems* 2–15 cm tall, usually with only a single node elevated above the base. *Leaves* short and fascicled (in clusters), the blades 1 mm or less broad, with short, inrolled prickle-pointed blades. *Sheaths* often with a tuft of long hairs at their base. *Spikelets* rather large, stalkless or short-stalked in a tight cluster, the inflorescence exceeded in length by the leaves of the cluster. *Spikelets* mostly 7–13 mm long and with six to twelve florets. *Glumes* about equal, with long, slender tips, or short-awned, about as long as the spikelet. *Lemmas* mostly 3–5 mm long, densely long-haired on the nerves, deeply cleft to just above the middle, and with a stout, straight or curved awn about as long as the lobes. Plants setting seed from June to November.

Fig. 75. Fluffgrass *(Erioneuron pulchellum)* plant.

DISTRIBUTION AND HABITAT. Fluffgrass occurs in the Trans-Pecos area of western Texas on dry, rocky slopes and desert flats, often in association with creosotebush.

USE. Although rather frequent on dry ranges of western Texas, fluffgrass is of poor forage value to both livestock and wildlife.

EUSTACHYS

76. **Stiffleaf eustachys** *Eustachys petraea* (Sw.) Desc. *(Chloris petraea Sw.)*

Perennial with stems in small clumps from a firm base, the plant often spreading by means of stout stolons. *Stems* mostly 20–120 cm tall, with the leaves clustered at the base. *Leaves* hairless, laterally compressed, the sheaths sharply keeled. *Blades* rather thick, abruptly pointed at the tip, up to 20 cm long and 3–7 mm broad. *Spikelets* closely placed and overlapping on two to eight unbranched, erect or spreading branches clustered at the tip of the stem, the branches 4–12 cm long. Spikelets two-flowered, the lower floret seed-producing and the upper one re-

Fig. 76.   Stiffleaf eustachys *(Eustachys petraea)* inflorescence and spikelet.

duced, often rudimentary. *Glumes* unequal, hairless, the first narrowly lanceolate, 0.9–1.5 mm long, and the second nearly linear, 1.1–1.7 mm long, and short-awned from a broad, lobed tip. *Lemma of lower floret* ovate to lanceolate, dark brown at maturity, 1.1–2.5 mm long and 0.2–0.5 mm wide, soft-haired on the upper one-half to three-fourths with hairs 0.1–0.4 mm long, the tip awnless or with a minute awn. *Upper (reduced) floret* cylindrical, hairless, 0.8–1 mm long, awnless or with a minute awn. Plants setting seed March through December.

DISTRIBUTION AND HABITAT. Stiffleaf eustachys is a familiar grass of the seashore, where it is common in beach sand and on the margins of brackish coastal waters. It is occasional in moist areas further inland.

USE. This grass is a native, warm-season perennial of no significance as a forage grass.

FESTUCA

77. Tall fescue   *Festuca arundinacea* Schreb.

Perennial bunch grass with stout, erect stems 50–150 cm (occasionally up to 200 cm) tall, often rough below the panicle. *Sheaths* rounded on the back, usually with thin, narrow, rounded auricles on either side at the

Fig. 77. Tall fescue *(Festuca arundinacea)* plant, spikelet, and floret.

tip. *Blades* elongate, flat or folded, 3–12 mm broad, often rough on the margins. *Panicles* mostly 10–30 cm long, erect or somewhat nodding, contracted and narrow to open, with the lower branches long and spreading. *Spikelets* breaking up between the florets, short-stalked and closely pressed against the branches, mostly 10–15 cm (sometimes up to 18 cm) long, with five to nine flowers. *Glumes* hairless, pointed, membranous on the margins, the first single-nerved, 4–6 mm long, and the second three-nerved, slightly longer than the first. *Lemmas* 6–9 mm long, rounded on the back, five-nerved, smooth or minutely roughened on the nerves, awnless or with an awn 1–4 mm long. *Paleas* as long as the lemmas, rough on the margins. Plants setting seed from April to June.

DISTRIBUTION AND HABITAT. Tall fescue is occasional in the northern and eastern counties of Texas. It is most frequent in seeded pastures or as a roadside escape in the vicinity of such pastures.

USE. An introduced, cool-season perennial native to Europe but now widely established in temperate and cool regions of North America, tall fescue provides good forage for livestock and wildlife but in Texas is significant mainly as an improved pasture grass. In our region it seldom persists under natural conditions.

HETEROPOGON

78. Tanglehead *Heteropogon contortus* (L.) Beauv. *ex* Roem. & Schult.

Tufted perennial with stems 20–80 cm tall, much branched at the base and also freely branching at the upper nodes with age. *Leaves* hairless except for a few long hairs on the sheath and blade margins near the ligule. *Sheaths* laterally compressed and sharply keeled. *Blades* flat, mostly 4–6 mm broad and 6–20 cm or more long. *Inflorescence* a stout raceme mostly 4–7 cm long, with the spikelets in pairs of one stalkless and one stalked. *Paired spikelets* on the lower part of the raceme with stamens only or neuter and awnless, with broad, thin, green, many-nerved, hairless or sparsely haired glumes. *Stalkless spikelets of upper spikelet pairs* 5–8 mm long, with a sharp-pointed, bearded base, rounded, dark-colored, several-nerved, brownish, with hairy glumes and a dark-colored, bent and twisted awn to 12 cm long. Plants setting seed mostly June through November, but occasionally March through December.

DISTRIBUTION AND HABITAT. Tanglehead occurs in central and western Texas and is frequent both in the grasslands of the lower Gulf Coast and in the mountains of western Texas, usually in sandy soil. It flowers March through December, mostly June through November.

USE. This grass is a native, warm-season perennial providing good grazing for livestock and poor grazing for wildlife. In some areas injury to sheep from the sharp-pointed, awned grains has been reported.

Fig. 78. Tanglehead *(Heteropogon contortus)* inflorescence and spikelet.

132 : Common Texas Grasses

HILARIA

Key to the species:
Base of plant not thick and hard, without rhizomes; slender, looping
    stolons typically developed ....
    .... Common curlymesquite, *H. belangeri*
Base of plant thick and hard, with stout, scaly rhizomes; slender, looping
    stolons not developed .... Tobosa, *H. mutica*

79. Common curlymesquite   *Hilaria belangeri* (Steud.) Nash

Low perennial with erect flowering stems 10–30 cm tall, these in
small tufts often at the nodes of wiry, widely spreading stolons. *Stem
nodes*, especially the lower ones, densely bearded with spreading hairs.
Blades short, flat or less commonly inrolled, often sparsely hairy, 1–2 mm
(occasionally up to 3 mm) broad. *Inflorescence* a spike mostly 2–3.5 cm
long, usually elevated on a slender stalk, the spikelets in clusters of three,
with four to eight spikelet clusters. *Spikelets* one- or two-flowered.
Glumes of lateral spikelets pale, united below, usually shorter than the
lemmas, the outer one slightly broadened above, notched or lobed, the
inner one shorter and narrower, and both frequently with the midnerve
extended into a bristle less than 1 mm long. *Glumes of central spikelet*
about equal, hairless, slightly broadened above, with awns mostly 2.5–5
mm long. *Lemma* thin, narrowed above, awnless. Plants setting seed
mostly August to October, but occasionally March to November.

DISTRIBUTION AND HABITAT. Common curlymesquite is found in all regions of the state except in the Post Oak Savanna and Pineywoods of
eastern Texas. It grows on rocky slopes, dry hillsides, and grassy or
brushy plains.

USE. A native, warm-season perennial providing fair grazing for livestock and for wildlife, common curlymesquite is grazed throughout the
year by horses, cattle, sheep, goats, deer, and antelope.

80. Tobosa   *Hilaria mutica* (Buckl.) Benth.

Perennial with tough or wiry stems 30–75 cm tall from a firm or hard,
usually rhizomatous base, often in pure stands and forming a sod. *Leaves*
hairless, the sheaths rounded on the back, the blades firm, flat or more
often inrolled, 2–4 mm broad. *Inflorescence* a tight spike mostly 4–8 cm
long and 6–8 mm thick. *Spikelets* in threes at each node, the spike with
eight to twenty-five closely placed, stalkless spikelet clusters. *Spikelet
clusters* mostly 6–9 mm long, with three spikelets nearly equal in length
and with a tuft of hairs 2–3 mm long at their base. *Glumes of lateral
spikelets* (with stamens only) broadened upward to a fan-shaped,
rounded, or abruptly "cut-off" (truncate) tip, densely or sparsely fringed
with hairs on the margins, the inner glumes with a rough or hairy awn
0.5–3 mm long on one side. *Glumes of central spikelet* narrow, usually

Fig. 79. Common curlymesquite *(Hilaria belangeri)* plant and two views of spikelet cluster.

short, irregularly cleft, and with awn-tipped nerves. *Lemmas* thin, undivided or irregularly dissected, fringed with hairs at the tip, and awnless or minutely awn-tipped. *Lemma and palea of central spikelet* mostly 5–6 mm long, with lateral margins more or less inrolled to form a tube through which the dark-colored stigmas protrude at flowering time. Plants setting seed April to August, occasionally to October.

DISTRIBUTION AND HABITAT. Tobosa grows throughout the western half of the state on dry, rocky slopes and dry upland plains and plateaus.

Fig. 80. Tobosa *(Hilaria mutica)*. Plant; *(above)* spikelet cluster; *(below)* spikelet cluster with one lateral spikelet removed.

USE. A native, warm-season perennial providing fair grazing for live-stock and poor grazing for wildlife, tobosa grass is grazed by both cattle and horses and makes good-quality hay if cut about the time that the spikes appear. Tobosa is a poor seed producer and spreads mostly from the rhizomes.

HORDEUM

Key to the species:

Lateral spikelets stalked; lemmas of the lateral spikelets absent or much smaller than the lemma of the central spikelet . . . .
. . . . Little barley, *H. pusillum*

Lateral spikelets and the central spikelet stalkless; lemmas of lateral spikelets as large as the lemma of the central spikelet . . . .
. . . . Barley, *H. vulgare*

81. Little barley *Hordeum pusillum* Nutt.

Tufted annual with erect or spreading stems mostly 10–40 cm tall. *Stem nodes* dark-colored, hairless. *Leaves* hairless or softly hairy. *Blades* flat, thin, mostly 3–12 cm long and 2–5 mm broad, occasionally with small auricles. *Inflorescence* narrow, dense, and spikelike, mostly 4–8 cm long and 4–8 mm broad without the awns. *Axis of inflorescence* breaking up at maturity, the short internodes falling attached to the spikelets. *Spikelets* single-flowered. *Outer glumes of lateral spikelets* bristlelike, without ex-panded bodies, the other glumes broadened and flattened above their base, with awns mostly 7–15 mm long. *Lemmas of lateral spikelets* short-awned, irregularly reduced, the body one-third to one-half as long as that of the central, seed-bearing spikelet. *Lemma of central spikelet* with a body usually 4–6 mm long and an awn 2–7 mm long. *Axis of spikelet* extended behind the palea as a stout bristle 2–4 mm long. Plants setting seed March to May or June.

DISTRIBUTION AND HABITAT. Little barley grows throughout the state, is locally frequent in early spring on disturbed pasture sites, roadways, and ditch banks, and is often associated with common sixweeksgrass (*Vulpia octoflora*) around anthills.

USE. This grass is a short-lived, cool season, native annual of essen-tially no value for livestock or wildlife grazing.

82. Barley *Hordeum vulgare* L.

Annual with thick, succulent stems mostly 50–120 cm tall. *Leaves* usually hairless. *Sheaths* thin, rounded on the back. *Blades* thin, flat, elongate, mostly 5–15 mm broad, usually with firm, well-developed auri-cles at their base. *Inflorescence* a thick, closely flowered spike 2–10 cm

Fig. 81.   Little barley (*Hordeum pusillum*) plant and joint of inflorescence main axis with spikelet cluster.

Fig. 82. Barley *(Hordeum vulgare)* inflorescence and spikelet cluster.

138 : Common Texas Grasses

long (excluding the awns), with three stalkless, seed-bearing, closely placed, single-flowered spikelets at each node of the axis. *Axis* not breaking up at maturity. *Glumes* flattened and slightly broadened at their base, hairless or variously hairy, tapering to a short or long awn. *Lemmas* shiny, mostly 8–12 mm long, in the usual cultivated varieties tapering to a stout, rough awn as much as 15 cm long. Plants setting seed mostly April to June.

DISTRIBUTION AND HABITAT. Barley is planted as a crop plant in many areas of the state and occasionally is present as a weed of roadsides and field borders; it does not persist out of cultivation.

USE. An introduced, cool-season annual, barley is valuable under cultivation as a forage plant for both livestock and wildlife.

KOELERIA

83. **Junegrass** *Koeleria pyramidata* (Lam.) Beauv. *(Koeleria cristata Pers.)*

Tufted perennial with stems 25–70 cm tall. *Leaves* mostly basal. *Sheaths* rounded on the back or somewhat keeled, the lowermost stiff-haired. *Blades* elongate, 1–4 mm broad, flat or irregularly folded, hairless to sparsely or strongly hairy on one or both surfaces. *Inflorescence* a contracted panicle 5–15 cm long, with short, erect, densely flowered branches. *Main panicle axis and branches* minutely hairy. *Spikelets* 4–5 mm long. *Glumes* large, roughened on the midnerve and back, slightly unequal, with the second obovate, about equaling the lowermost lemma. *Lemmas* rough or smooth and shiny on the back, pointed at the tip. *Palea* translucent and shiny, as large as the lemma. Plants setting seed mostly April to June.

DISTRIBUTION AND HABITAT. Junegrass is occasional in grasslands of north central and western Texas, mostly on rocky slopes of rough, broken country and often in partial shade.

USE. Junegrass is a good native, cool-season, perennial forage grass that is widely distributed in western North America. This plant, however, is relatively infrequent in Texas and is of minor importance for forage.

LEERSIA

84. **Rice cutgrass** *Leersia oryzoides* (L.) Sw.

Tall, slender perennial with stems mostly 80–150 cm tall. A bunch grass that often curves upward from a spreading base and develops creeping rhizomes and stolons. *Stem nodes* with stiff hairs bent downwards. *Sheaths and blades* sharply rough to the touch, the margins and blade midnerve sharply saw-toothed. *Blades* long, mostly 7–10 mm broad, thin

Fig. 83. Junegrass (*Koeleria pyramidata*) plant and spikelet.

but firm. *Panicle* large, open, usually drooping, mostly 10–20 cm long.
Lower branches of panicle bare of spikelets for the lower 1.5–4 cm.
Spikelets single-flowered, awnless, narrowly oblong, 4–5.5 mm long and
1.5–2 mm broad, asymmetrical, clustered on short stalks at the branch
tips. *Glumes* absent. *Lemmas* firm, laterally flattened and keeled, boat-
shaped, five-nerved, the lemma and palea fringed with stiff bristles on the
keels. Plants setting seed mostly April to November.

140 : Common Texas Grasses

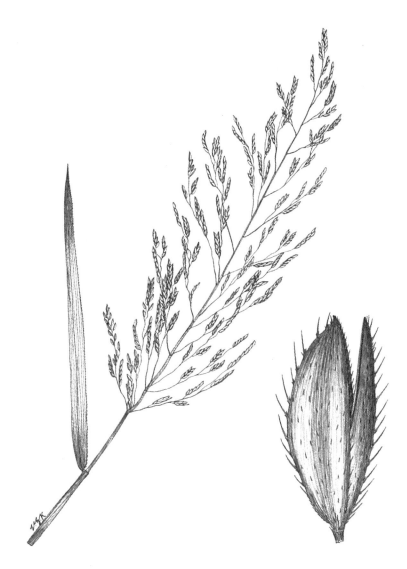

Fig. 84. Rice cutgrass *(Leersia oryzoides)* inflorescence and spikelet.

DISTRIBUTION AND HABITAT. Rice cutgrass is occasional throughout the state, except perhaps in the High Plains, and grows mostly in saturated soils along lakes, rivers, marshes, and wet ditches.

USE. A rather coarse native, perennial, warm-season bunch grass with sharply toothed leaf margins, rice cutgrass provides little if any forage for livestock but provides habitat and feed (grain) for ducks and other game birds.

Accounts of the Grasses : 141

LEPTOCHLOA

Key to the species:

Lemmas broad, usually notched at the tip, the lower lemmas 3.5–5 mm
      long; plants perennial . . . . Green sprangletop, *L. dubia*
Lemmas narrowly or broadly pointed at the tip, the lower lemmas 1–1.6
      mm long; plants annual . . . . Red sprangletop, *L. filiformis*

Fig. 85.   Green sprangletop *(Leptochloa dubia)* plant and spikelet.

85. Green sprangletop *Leptochloa dubia* (H.B.K.) Nees

Tufted perennial with stems mostly 30–110 cm tall, unbranched above base, without stolons or rhizomes. *Sheaths* hairless or the lower ones soft-haired, the lower sheaths, especially those of sterile shoots, often laterally flattened and sharply keeled. *Blades* dull bluish green, hairless, rough or sparsely hairy, mostly 5–30 cm long and 2–7 mm broad, often inrolled when dried. *Inflorescence* with two to ten (occasionally up to fifteen) unbranched primary branches scattered along the main axis, the branches mostly 4–12 cm long, slender, loosely erect or spreading. *Spikelets* almost stalkless, solitary at the nodes, loosely to closely overlapping on the branch axis, with usually three to eight florets. *Glumes* lanceolate, awnless, the second 4–5 mm long and the first slightly shorter. *Lemmas* broad, rounded on the back, truncate (chopped off) and usually notched at the tip, hairless or hairy on the margins, the lowermost 3.5–5 mm long. Plants setting seed mostly May to November.

DISTRIBUTION AND HABITAT. Green sprangletop grows in all regions of Texas except the Pineywoods and the Post Oak Savanna, but it is most common in southern and western Texas, growing mainly on loose, rocky, well-drained soils.

USE. A native, warm-season perennial that provides good grazing for livestock and fair grazing for wildlife, green sprangletop is highly palatable but seldom grows in pure stands and usually is associated with other native perennial grasses. It is the best forage species of the sprangletops. It regularly develops highly fertile self-fertilized spikelets in the protection of the lower leaf sheaths.

86. Red sprangletop *Leptochloa filiformis* (Lam.) Beauv.

Annual with slender, spreading and upward-curving, much-branched stems 10–80 cm tall. *Leaves* usually hairy. *Sheaths* rounded on the back. *Blades* long, thin, flat, 2–10 mm broad. *Inflorescence* long and narrow, usually one-third to one-half the entire stem length. *Inflorescence branches* few to numerous, scattered on the upper portion of the stem, slender, flexuous, mostly 3–10 cm long and 1–2 mm thick, erect to spreading or widely spreading at maturity. *Spikelets* with two to four flowers, 1.5–3 mm long, widely spaced on the branch axis and only slightly overlapping. *Glumes* thin, pointed, the first narrower and usually slightly shorter than the second and the second as long as the spikelet. *Lemmas* mostly 1–1.6 mm long, three-nerved, usually but not always hairy on the nerves below the middle, rounded at the tip. *Grain* usually 0.7–0.8 mm long. Plants setting seed mostly July to November but occasionally as early as May.

DISTRIBUTION AND HABITAT. Found throughout Texas except on the High Plains, red sprangletop grows mostly as a weed in the disturbed soils of flower beds, gardens, ditches, disturbed pastures, and roadways.

Fig. 86. Red sprangletop *(Leptochloa filiformis)* inflorescence and spikelet.

144 : Common Texas Grasses

USE. This weedy, native, warm-season annual is of no significance as a forage grass.

LEPTOLOMA

87. Fall witchgrass *Leptoloma cognatum* (Schult.) Chase

Perennial with a knotty, hairy, rhizomatous base, and with open panicles of spikelets on long, slender, spreading branches and spikelet stalks. *Stems* mostly 30–80 cm tall, much-branched at the base and middle stem nodes to produce many secondary panicles in addition to the primary one. *Blades* thin, short, flat, usually wavy on the margins. *Base of spikelet and base of panicle* breaking off to become a tumbleweed. *Spikelets* 2.5–4 mm long, two-flowered, the lower floret with stamens only or neuter and the upper floret seed-bearing. *Glumes and lemmas* awnless, the first glume absent or vestigial and the second with three to five nerves, about equaling the lemma of the lower floret, with five to seven nerves. *Second glume and lemma of lower floret* densely covered with long, soft hairs to nearly hairless between the nerves and on the margins. *Lemma of upper floret* dark brown, smooth, leathery, narrowly pointed, with thin, flat (not inrolled) margins. Plants setting seed mostly May to November but occasionally as early as February.

DISTRIBUTION AND HABITAT. Fall witchgrass occurs throughout the state in open or partially wooded pastures and rangelands on both clayey and sandy soils.

USE. A native, warm-season perennial that provides fair grazing for livestock and for wildlife, this relatively inconspicuous grass probably produces more forage than is generally recognized. Although it grows rapidly and seeds readily, fall witchgrass has a weak root system and is relatively short-lived.

LIMNODEA

88. Ozarkgrass *Limnodea arkansana* (Nutt.) L. H. Dewey

Short-lived annual with weak stems, thin, flat blades, and a contracted panicle of single-flowered spikelets. *Stems* in small clumps, mostly 20–50 cm tall, but occasionally taller. *Sheaths* rounded on the back, often hairy. *Blades* hairless or more commonly hairy on both surfaces, 2–8 mm broad and 3–12 cm long. *Panicles* narrow, contracted, 5–20 cm long, with few to several short branches, these mostly bearing spikelets to their base or nearly so. *Spikelets* 3.5–4 mm long excluding the awn, breaking off below the glumes. *Glumes* equal, as long as the spikelet, firm, with three to five obscure nerves, rounded and minutely roughened on the back, usually hairy but becoming hairless, with an awnless, pointed tip. *Lemma*

Fig. 87. Fall witchgrass *(Leptoloma cognatum)* plant and spikelet.

146 : Common Texas Grasses

Fig. 88. Ozarkgrass *(Limnodea arkansana)* inflorescence and spikelet.

about as long as the glumes, hairless and rough, with a twisted and bent awn attached just below the pointed or minutely forked tip. *Lemma awn* mostly 8–11 mm long. *Palea* thin, narrow, shorter than the lemma. Plants setting seed mostly late March to early June.

DISTRIBUTION AND HABITAT. Found throughout the state except in the far west, this species is a common grass of open woodlands, stream and ditch banks, and brushy grasslands.

USE. Ozarkgrass is a short-lived native spring annual of little or no significance as a forage grass.

LOLIUM

Key to the species:
Glume shorter than the spikelet; long-lived annual or short-lived perennial .... Ryegrass, *L. perenne*
Glume longer than the uppermost floret; short-lived annual ....
.... Darnel, *L. temulentum*

89. Ryegrass (perennial ryegrass; Italian ryegrass)   *Lolium perenne* L.
    Tufted annual or short-lived perennial. *Stems* 25–70 cm tall, thick and succulent when green. *Leaves* hairless, dark green. *Sheaths* often with delicate, membranous auricles. *Upper margins of sheath* thin, extending upward at the base of the blade to form a membranous ligule. *Blades* 2–10 mm broad, shriveling and with very little body when dry. *Inflorescence* a spike 10–20 cm long and with fifteen to thirty spikelets borne singly at the nodes. *Spikelets* mostly with five to twelve flowers, oriented edgewise to the central axis, the first glume absent except on the terminal spikelet. *Glumes* mostly 5–10 mm long, one-third to two-thirds as long as the spikelet. *Lemmas* about as long as the glumes, awnless and with a blunt, membranous tip or with an awn up to 8 mm long from a minutely notched tip. Plants setting seed March to June.
    DISTRIBUTION AND HABITAT. Ryegrass occurs nearly throughout the state but is apparently absent from the southern portion of the South Texas Plains. It is a European species which was brought into the United States as a pasture grass at an early date and is now widespread throughout the country, especially in the northern states.
    USE. Ryegrass is an introduced, cool-season perennial or long-lived annual that provides good grazing for livestock and poor grazing for wildlife. Occasionally seeded in pastures and as a cool-season lawn grass, it is a common weed of roadsides, field borders, and ditches throughout the state. Ryegrass was the first pasture grass to be cultivated in Europe, and numerous strains or commercial varieties have been developed. Often recognized as a distinct species, *L. multiflorum* Lam., Italian ryegrass, is one of the forms with awned spikelets.

90. Darnel   *Lolium temulentum* L.
    Annual with thick, weak stems mostly 30–70 cm tall. *Leaves* hairless, typically with sheath auricles. *Blades* thin, flat, 2–8 mm broad. *Inflorescence* a slender, stiffly erect spike 10–25 cm long, the spikelets closely pressed against the flattened and somewhat hollowed-out axis joints. *Spikelets* laterally flattened and oriented edgewise to the axis, mostly with five to nine florets. *First glume* absent except on the terminal floret, the second glume broad, 1.5–2 cm long, with five to thirteen nerves, pointed or rounded at the tip. *Lemmas* 4–7 mm long, smooth or rough, and with awns 5–15 mm long or awnless. Plants setting seed March to May.

Fig. 89.   Ryegrass *(Lolium perenne)* inflorescence, spikelet with awnless lemmas (left), and spikelet with awned lemmas (right).

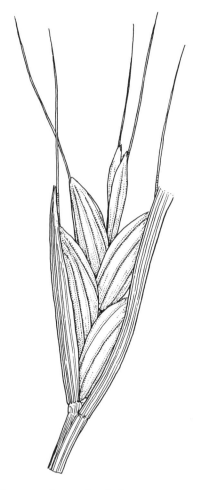

Fig. 90.   Darnel *(Lolium temulentum)* spikelet.

DISTRIBUTION AND HABITAT. Darnel is found growing in all regions of
the state except the extreme western portion as a weed of roadsides,
disturbed fields, and waste places. It is a European weed now widespread
in the United States.

USE. Darnel has been known as a poisonous weed of cultivated fields
since the earliest historical periods. Like the classical cheat grass or
brome grass, *Bromus secalinus* L., it was thought to be a degenerate form
of rye and other cereals. The poisonous properties of darnel are now
known to be due to the presence in the grain of a fungus which produces a
deadly poisonous alkaloid, temulin. Infected grains have been found in an
Egyptian tomb believed to date from 2000 B.C. Awnless forms of darnel
are classified as *L. temulentum* var. *leptochaetium* A. Br.

MELICA

Key to the species:

Panicle simple, the branches rarely rebranched; rudiment (upper reduced floret or florets) usually bent at an angle to the spikelet axis; tips of the two lower seed-bearing florets nearly at the same height .... Twoflower melic, *M. mutica*

Panicle usually with rebranched primary branches, the branches spreading; rudiment never bent at an angle to the spikelet axis; tip of the second seed-bearing floret 1–2 mm higher than the tip of the lowermost floret .... Threeflower melic, *M. nitens*

91. Twoflower melic   *Melica mutica* Walt.

Slender, tufted perennial with stems mostly 45–100 cm tall from creeping rhizomes. *Sheaths* rough or hairy, the margins fused together and the sheath cylindrical nearly to the tip on the upper leaves. *Blades* thin, hairless to short-haired, flat or folded, elongate, 2–6 mm broad. *Inflorescence* usually a simple narrow panicle or raceme 4–16 cm long, the primary branches infrequently rebranched. *Spikelets* 7–11 mm long, flat-topped and more or less triangular in outline, with two (rarely more) perfect (bisexual) florets, the lower longer than the upper and the tips at about the same height. *Glumes* equal or the second slightly longer, mostly 6–9 mm long, and both thin and hairless, with thin margins and tip. *Lemmas* firm, minutely roughened, with narrow, thin margins and a broad, thin tip. *Lemma of lower floret* 6–10 mm long, the lemma of the second floret shorter. *Grain* 2–3 mm long. *Upper florets* reduced to a sterile rudiment, this obconic and truncate (chopped off) at the tip, at maturity spreading at an angle from the spikelet axis. Plants setting seed March to May.

DISTRIBUTION AND HABITAT. Twoflower melic grows in the Pineywoods and Post Oak Savanna of eastern Texas in moist openings in woods, along riverbanks, and in low pastures. It is rather frequent but seldom abundant.

USE. A native, cool-season perennial, this grass is highly palatable to livestock and wildlife but seldom sufficiently abundant to provide much forage.

92. Threeflower melic   *Melica nitens* (Scribn.) Nutt. *ex* Piper

Stems mostly 50–120 cm tall in small clumps from a firm base forming rhizomes. *Sheaths* hairless or minutely hairy, the margins fused together to form a tubular sheath nearly to the top. *Ligules* membranous, mostly 3–6 mm long. *Blades* hairless or minutely hairy, flat, 3–10 mm (or as much as 15 mm) broad. *Inflorescence* a more or less open panicle, usually 10–26 cm long but occasionally shorter, the lower branches usually rebranched, spreading or ascending. *Spikelets* 8–15 mm long, with

Fig. 91. Twoflower melic *(Melica mutica)* inflorescence and spikelet.

one to four seed-bearing florets, these erect or nearly so at maturity, the tip of the second floret exceeding the tip of the first by 1–2 mm. *Glumes* shorter than the spikelet, broadly or narrowly pointed, thin on the margins and at the tip. *First glume* usually broad, 5–7 mm long, and the second glume narrower, 7–9 mm long. *Lemmas* minutely roughened, with thin, narrow margins and a broadly or narrowly pointed tip. *Lemma of lower floret* 8–11 mm long. *Upper floret or florets* reduced and rudimentary, forming an oblong or obovate rudiment, usually broadest

Fig. 92. Threeflower melic *(Melica nitens)* plant and spikelets.

near the tip, erect and not bent at an angle from the spikelet axis. Plants setting seed mostly May to June.

DISTRIBUTION AND HABITAT. Threeflower melic grows in the central and western regions of the state on relatively undisturbed sites in open woodlands, moist canyon slopes and valley bottoms, and rocky pasturelands.

USE. This grass is a native, cool-season perennial that is highly palatable to livestock and wildlife but seldom grows in dense stands or contributes a great amount of forage. Threeflower melic frequently is confused with twoflower melic, from which it differs in its more woody plant base, generally taller and coarser stems, longer ligules, often broader blades, larger panicles with rebranched lower branches, narrower and longer spikelets, and rudiment that is not cone-shaped and does not spread at an angle from the spikelet axis. In Texas plants of both species, the spikelets quite regularly have two perfect florets, and thus the name threeflower melic is often misleading.

MUHLENBERGIA

Key to the species:

Spikelet stalks 5–20 mm long, the spikelets widely spaced in a loose, open panicle . . . . Bush muhly, *M. porteri*
Spikelet stalks 0.5–3 mm long, the spikelets closely pressed around a few short branches of a narrow, contracted panicle . . . .
. . . . Nimblewill, *M. schreberi*

93. Bush muhly *Muhlenbergia porteri* Scribn. *ex* Beal

Perennial with slender, wiry, much-branched stems from a hard, knotty base. *Stems* mostly 30–100 cm long, with numerous nodes and short internodes, often minutely hairy just below the nodes. *Sheaths* mostly shorter than the internodes. *Blades* thin and short, becoming inrolled and soon lost from the plant, mostly 2–5 cm long and 0.5–2 mm broad. *Panicles* small and numerous on the much-branched stems, mostly 4–10 cm long and nearly as broad, usually purple. *Spikelets* widely spaced on stalks 5–20 mm long. *Glumes* thin, hairless, narrowly lanceolate, about equal, 2–3 mm long, shorter than the lemma. *Lemmas* thin, three-nerved, usually sparsely hairy between the nerves and on the lateral margins, with a body 3–4 mm long and an awn 5–12 mm long. *Paleas* about as long as the lemmas, tapering to a narrow tip. Plants setting seed June to November.

DISTRIBUTION AND HABITAT. Bush muhly is found in the western portion of the state on dry, rocky slopes, on brushy flats, and along dry arroyos, usually in the protection of shrubs or cacti.

Fig. 93. Bush muhly *(Muhlenbergia porteri)* plant and spikelet with floret separated from glumes.

USE. A native, warm-season perennial providing good grazing for livestock and poor grazing for wildlife, bush muhly is eagerly sought out by cattle and under heavy grazing pressure persists only in the protection of cacti and spiny shrubs.

Fig. 94. Nimblewill *(Muhlenbergia schreberi)* plant and spikelet.

94. Nimblewill *Muhlenbergia schreberi* Gmel.

Low, creeping perennial with slender, spreading, much-branched stems that usually form stolons and root at the lower nodes. *Flowering stems* mostly 10–40 cm (rarely up to 60 cm) tall. *Sheaths* shorter than the internodes, typically hairless except for a few long hairs on the upper margins and near the throat. *Blades* thin, flat, hairless or with a few hairs above the ligule, mostly 3–8 cm long and 1–3 mm broad. *Panicles* small and contracted, usually lobed or interrupted, mostly 4–13 cm long and 1–4 mm wide, the short panicle branches commonly closely pressed to the stem but sometimes slightly spreading. *Spikelet stalks* appressed, mostly shorter than the spikelets. *Glumes* rounded at the tip, the first often rudimentary or absent and the second 0.1–0.3 mm long. *Lemmas* 2–2.5 mm long, with an awn about 1.5–5 mm long, the body usually thinly haired at the base with rather coarse hairs. Plants setting seed May to November.

DISTRIBUTION AND HABITAT. Nimblewill occurs throughout the eastern, central, and north-central portions of the state, usually in the partial shade of trees, bushes, or rocky banks, on soils that are moist much of the time.

USE. A native, warm-season perennial that provides fair forage for livestock and wildlife in shaded sites in woodland or brushy pastures, nimblewill often takes on the aspect of tall bermudagrass in open but shaded sites. It is, however, more delicate and much less aggressive than bermudagrass.

ORYZA

95. Rice *Oryza sativa* L.

Tufted annual with weak, stiffly erect culms mostly 80–160 cm tall, in small clusters or clumps. *Sheaths* hairless or the lower ones sparsely hairy, usually with well-developed auricles that are rounded or elongate and tapering to a point, occasionally bearing one to four stiff hairs. *Ligules* large, thick, two-lobed, the lobes 5–15 mm long on the lower leaves. *Blades* hairless, 0.7–2 cm broad, flat or folded, those of the lower leaves often greatly thickened in the vicinity of the midrib. *Inflorescence* a somewhat contracted, drooping panicle with large, one-flowered spikelets. *Panicle branches and spikelet stalks* hairless or sparsely hairy, breaking off below the spikelet. *Spikelets* single-flowered, mostly 7–10 mm long, flattened laterally, with two short, pointed, glumelike structures below the lemma. *Lemma and palea* firm, finely roughened, keel-shaped, of equal length, but the lemmas broader. *Lemmas* awnless or with a stout awn, with three to five nerves, two of which are on the margins. *Paleas* two-nerved, the nerves on the extreme margins. Plants setting seed June to December.

Fig. 95. Rice *(Oryza sativa)* inflorescence and spikelet.

DISTRIBUTION AND HABITAT. Rice is a cultivated crop plant on the Texas coastal plain, and it occasionally grows as an escape in moist, disturbed soils in the eastern portion of the state. It is cultivated throughout the warmer areas of the world.

USE. Rice is used only incidentally as an animal forage plant, although it is palatable to livestock. Wild geese and ducks feed extensively on rice seedlings and on regrowth following the seed harvest in the fall.

PANICUM

Key to the species:

Plants annual .... Common witchgrass, *P. capillare*

Plants perennial

First glume about as long as the second glume, broad and rounded at the tip .... Vinemesquite, *P. obtusum*

First glume shorter than the second glume, or if nearly as long, then pointed at the tip

Spikelets 4 mm or more long; plants tall and coarse, with rhizomes or stolons

Plants of saline coastal sands; panicles tightly contracted .... Bitter panicum, *P. amarum*

Plants not of saline coastal sands; panicles not tightly contracted .... Switchgrass, *P. virgatum*

Spikelets less than 4 mm long; plants variable in habit

Palea of lower floret firm, enlarged and inflated, spreading the spikelet at maturity; low, tufted weak perennial without rhizomes or stolons .... Gaping panicum, *P. hians*

Palea of lower floret not firm, not enlarged and inflated, not spreading the spikelet at maturity

Stems tall, hard and woody, becoming much-branched above .... Blue panicum, *P. antidotale*

Stems tall or short, not becoming woody or much-branched above

Thick, scaly, creeping rhizomes developed; lower stem internodes and sheaths laterally compressed and keeled

Spikelets 2.4–2.6 mm long; lemma of the upper (seed-bearing) floret thin ..... Maidencane, *P. hemitomon*

Spikelets 2.8–3.5 mm long; lemma of the upper (seed-bearing) floret thick .... Beaked panicum, *P. anceps*

Thick, scaly, creeping rhizomes not developed; lower stem internodes and sheaths rounded

Lower floret male (with stamens only) .... Kleingrass, *P. coloratum*

Lower floret neuter .... *P. hallii*

96. Bitter panicum *Panicum amarum* Ell.

Coarse perennial with hairless stems covered by a whitish waxy coating, in large or small clumps or solitary from stout, creeping rhizomes. *Stems* 0.3–2 m or more tall, usually bending upward from a spreading base. *Leaves* firm, with a whitish waxy coating, usually hairless except for the ligular hairs. *Sheaths* rounded. *Blades* flat or folded, elongate, mostly 3–15 mm broad. *Inflorescence* a dense, contracted panicle 10–40 cm long. *Panicle branches, branchlets and spikelet stalks* hairless, the stalks

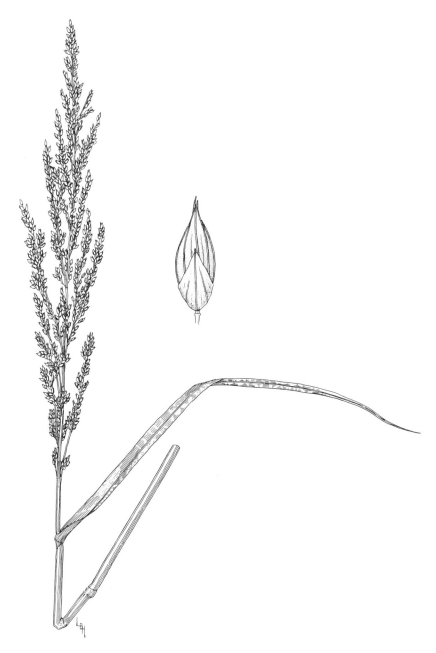

Fig. 96. Bitter panicum *(Panicum amarum)* inflorescence and spikelet.

short and stout. *Spikelets* mostly 4.5–6 mm long, hairless. *Glumes* pointed, the first one-half to two-thirds as long as the second and the second slightly exceeding the lower lemma, usually narrow and appearing somewhat beaked at the tip. *Lower floret* with stamens only, with the palea slightly shorter than the lemma. *Lemma of upper (seed-bearing) floret* smooth and shiny, ovate or oblong. Plants setting seed mostly September to November.

DISTRIBUTION AND HABITAT. This grass grows on sandy beaches and dunes along the Gulf Coast.

USE. Bitter panicum is a familiar native, warm-season bunch grass of coastal areas that often forms rather extensive colonies at the edge of the dunes. It has little if any value as a forage grass.

Fig. 97.   Beaked panicum *(Panicum anceps)* inflorescence, spikelet, and floret.

97. Beaked panicum   *Panicum anceps* Michx.

Perennial with tufted stems 30–100 cm tall from stout, scaly rhizomes. *Stem bases* flattened, often keeled, usually curving upward from a spreading base. *Stem nodes* hairless or somewhat hairy. *Leaves* hairless, rough, or variously hairy or downy. In the more hairy forms, the collar and sheath base usually densely stiff-haired. *Lower sheaths* typically keeled and laterally compressed. *Blades* long and narrow, flat or folded, 4–8 mm broad. *Panicles* variable, open or somewhat contracted, 15–40 cm long, with spikelets short-stalked and clustered on secondary branches, branchlets, and tips of primary branches; lower panicle branches mostly 4–15 cm long. *Spikelets* hairless, rough on the keel of the first glume, 2.8–3.5 mm long, oriented slightly at an angle to the stalk. *First glume* broad, broadly pointed at the tip, one-third to one-half as long as the spikelet. *Second glume and lemma of lower floret* about equal, narrowly pointed, rather widely separated at maturity. *Upper floret* about 1 mm shorter than second glume and lower lemma, the lemma narrowly oblong, smooth, and shiny. Plants flowering July through November.

DISTRIBUTION AND HABITAT. Beaked panicum is found in the eastern one-third of the state, mostly along creeks or riverbanks in forests or shaded, grassy pasturelands and usually in low, sandy, moist areas.

USE. This grass is a native, warm-season perennial that provides good grazing for livestock and fair grazing for wildlife.

98. Blue panicum *Panicum antidotale* Retz.

Tall, bushy perennial with stout stems and a hard, knotty base. *Stems* mostly 0.6–2.5 m tall, often with a whitish waxy coating, becoming much branched and bushy in age. *Stem nodes* hairy, conspicuously swollen. *Sheaths* hairless or the collar minutely downy. *Blades* flat, elongate, hairless, or the lower ones minutely downy, mostly 4–12 mm broad. *Panicles* open or somewhat dense and contracted, freely branched, mostly 12–25 cm long. *Spikelets* hairless, awnless, broadly ovate, 2.5–3 mm long, borne on short stalks and at the tips of short branchlets. *First glume* thin, broad, broadly rounded or broad and pointed at the tip, mostly one-third to one-half the length of the spikelet. *Second glume and lemma of lower floret* about equal, broad and thin at the tip. *Lower floret* with stamens only, with a palea as long and nearly as large as the lemma. *Lemma of upper (seed-bearing) floret* smooth, shiny, narrowly pointed, about as long as the spikelet. Plants setting seed April to November or December.

DISTRIBUTION AND HABITAT. Blue panicum is commonly used in range reseeding following brush control in central Texas, especially in the southern portion. It commonly persists for several years following establishment, but in time it usually diminishes in stand.

USE. This introduced, warm-season perennial provides good grazing for both livestock and wildlife. It reportedly can be the cause of prussic acid poisoning in livestock under certain conditions of growth.

99. Common witchgrass *Panicum capillare* L.

Spreading, weak-stemmed annual. *Stems* usually 20–80 cm long but much shorter on stunted plants, much-branched and spreading at the base, hairy at least at the nodes. *Sheaths* with stiff, spreading hairs. *Blades* flat, elongate, 5–15 mm broad, hairy on one or both surfaces or merely haired on the lower margins. *Panicle* large, diffusely branched, usually half or more as broad as long and often half or more as long as the

Fig. 98.   Blue panicum *(Panicum antidotale)* plant and spikelet.

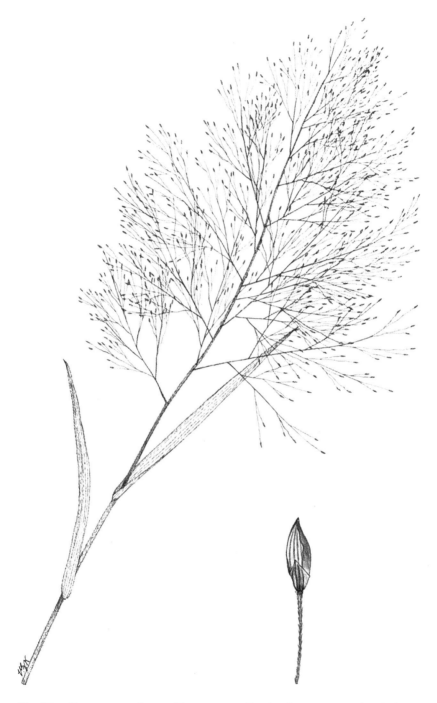

Fig. 99.   Common witchgrass *(Panicum capillare)* inflorescence and spikelet.

164 : Common Texas Grasses

stem, the branches widely spreading at maturity, hairy in the angle between branch and stem. *Spikelets* widely spaced on their stalks, mostly 1–3 cm or more long, infrequently overlapping. *Panicle* breaking off and rolling as a tumbleweed at maturity. *Spikelets* hairless, 2–3.5 mm long, the tips of the upper glume and lower lemma rather abruptly extended into a long-pointed tip. *First glume* short- or long-pointed, one-third to two-thirds as long as the spikelet. *Palea of lower floret* typically absent but occasionally developed. *Lemma of upper (seed-bearing) floret* firm, smooth and shiny, 1.3–2.3 mm long, 0.5–0.9 mm broad. Plants setting seed June or July to November.

DISTRIBUTION AND HABITAT. Occasional in all regions of the state except the South Texas Plains, common witchgrass is usually found in north-central Texas, where it grows as a weed of disturbed soils, often in gardens, flower beds, vacant lots, and roadsides.

USE. This species is a native, warm-season, weedy annual with no significance as a forage grass.

100. Kleingrass *Panicum coloratum* L.

Tufted, leafy, erect perennial with stems mostly 60–135 cm tall from firm, often knotty bases. *Rhizomes or stolons* not developed. *Stem nodes* hairless or minutely downy. *Sheaths* hairless or hairy with stiff, swollen-based hairs. *Blades* flat, elongate, 2–6 mm (occasionally up to 8 mm) broad, hairless or finely hairy on one or both surfaces. *Inflorescence* an open panicle mostly 8–25 cm long, with spikelets short-stalked on spreading, freely rebranched branches. *Spikelets* 2.8–3.2 mm long, hairless. *First glume* 1–1.5 mm long, broad at the base, abruptly narrowing to a point. *Second glume and lemma of lower floret* about equal, or the narrowly pointed second glume longer. *Lower floret* with stamens and a large, broad, thin palea. *Lemma of upper (seed-bearing) floret* hard, smooth and shiny, slightly beaked at the tip. Plants setting seed mostly May to September.

DISTRIBUTION AND HABITAT. Kleingrass has been introduced into southern and central Texas as a forage grass, and it persists on ranges of the Edwards Plateau (central Texas). It is native to Africa.

USE. This species is an introduced, perennial, warm-season forage grass that provides good grazing for livestock.

101. *Panicum hallii* Vasey

Perennial with erect or ascending stiff stems covered with a whitish waxy coating, 20–80 cm tall. *Stem nodes* hairless or with closely pressed fine down. *Blades* flat, the lower ones sometimes weak and curling when dried, nearly hairless or sparsely hairy with stiff, swollen-based hairs, 4–30 cm long, and 2–10 mm broad. *Sheaths* mostly equaling but somewhat shorter than the internodes, sparsely hairy to hairless. *Panicles*

Fig. 100. Kleingrass *(Panicum coloratum)* plant and spikelet.

moderately large, usually well projecting, pyramidal, with few to many branches. *Spikelets* hairless, long- or short-pointed, 2.2–3.7 mm long. *First glume* one-third to two-thirds the length of the spikelet, pointed at the tip. *Second glume and lemma of lower floret* about equal and as long as the spikelet. *Lemma and palea* of upper floret dark brown and shiny, ovate-elliptic. Plants setting seed April to November.

166 : Common Texas Grasses

Fig. 101a.   Hall panicum (*Panicum hallii* var. *hallii*) plant, spikelet, and floret.

Accounts of the Grasses : 167

Fig. 101b.   Filly panicum *(Panicum hallii* var. *filipes)* plant and spikelet.

Key to the varieties:

Primary panicle branches mostly fewer than fifteen, few-flowered, with spikelets closely appressed near the ends of stiffly ascending branches; sheaths mostly with swollen-based hairs; stem nodes downy . . . . Hall panicum, *P. hallii* var. *hallii*

Primary panicle branches mostly more than fifteen, many-flowered, with spikelets closely pressed against branchlets or more commonly somewhat spreading on slender stalks; sheaths hairless or sometimes hairy near the tip; stem nodes with short hairs or hairless . . . . Filly panicum, *P. hallii* var. *filipes*

101a. Hall panicum *Panicum hallii* Vasey var. *hallii*

DISTRIBUTION AND HABITAT. This grass occurs throughout the state except in the Pineywoods. It is scattered to abundant on sandy to clayey calcareous soils.

USE. Hall panicum is a native, warm-season perennial providing fair grazing for livestock and wildlife.

101b. Filly panicum *Panicum hallii* Vasey var. *filipes* (Scribn.) Waller

DISTRIBUTION AND HABITAT. Filly panicum grows throughout the state except in the Pineywoods. It is occasional to frequent along moist roadsides and disturbed sites on clay soils.

USE. Filly panicum, like Hall panicum, provides fair grazing for livestock and wildlife. This variety (var. *filipes*) can usually be distinguished from var. *hallii* by its taller habit, weak instead of stiff or curled blades, larger panicles with more branches and spikelets, and smaller spikelets. Filly panicum is most common in southern Texas, where it grows as a tall, hairless, purplish plant, often with a whitish waxy coating, with large, many-branched panicles having slender, spreading branches.

102. Maidencane *Panicum hemitomon* Schult.

Strong perennial with erect stems usually forming large colonies from creeping rhizomes and stolons. *Stems* mostly 50–150 cm tall, with numerous sterile shoots associated with the relatively few flowering shoots. *Sterile shoots* sometimes with densely hairy sheaths. *Flowering shoots* usually with hairless sheaths. *Blades* of erect stems flat, lanceolate, mostly 12–30 cm long and 7–15 mm broad, typically hairless. *Panicles* contracted, mostly 10–30 cm long and seldom over 1.5 cm broad, the spikelets closely clustered on erect, short or rather long primary branches and short, closely pressed secondary branches. *Primary branches* bearing spikelets to the base, usually with a tuft of silvery hairs below and a few long hairs at the bases of the secondary branches. *Spikelets* with very short stalks. *Glumes* rough on the midnerve and often beaked at the tip. *First glume* pointed, about half as long as the spikelet, the second glume

Fig. 102. Maidencane *(Panicum hemitomon)* plant and spikelet.

equaling the lower lemma or slightly shorter. *Lower floret* with stamens only, with a thin palea slightly shorter than the lemma. *Lemma and palea of upper (seed-bearing) floret* shiny, relatively thin, the lemma only loosely clasping the palea. Plants setting seed mostly April to September.

DISTRIBUTION AND HABITAT. Maidencane grows mostly in the Pineywoods of eastern Texas and along the Gulf coastal plain in ditches and along canals, edges of swales, riverbanks, and lakeshores.

USE. This native, warm-season perennial provides good grazing for livestock and fair grazing for wildlife.

103. Gaping panicum *Panicum hians* Ell.
Perennial with slender, tufted stems mostly 20–75 cm tall, these strictly erect or more commonly curving upward from a reclining base, often freely branched. *Nodes* hairless, often rough. *Leaves and stems* bright green. *Sheaths* rounded or somewhat compressed laterally, hairless or fringed with down on the upper margins. *Blades* flat or folded, narrow, mostly 6–18 cm long and 2–5 mm broad, often hairy with soft or harsh hairs above the ligule on the upper surface. *Panicles* small, few-flowered, 6–20 cm long. *Panicle branching* variable, mostly with spikelets clustered along erect or spreading short or long primary branches and short secondary branches. *Primary branches* slender, usually bare of spikelets on the lower 1.5–3 cm. *Spikelets* hairless, 1.8–2.6 mm long, at first broadly oblong, later widely gaping between the florets. *First glume* pointed, one-third to one-half as long as the spikelet. *Second glume* equaling or slightly shorter than the lemma of the lower floret. *Lower floret* neuter, the palea becoming firm, swollen, often terminating in a small, short point, much larger and broader than the lemma. *Lemma of upper (seed-bearing) floret* narrowly ovate, pointed, smooth but not shiny. Plants setting seed mostly December through May, but occasionally flowering throughout the year.

DISTRIBUTION AND HABITAT. This grass is found in the eastern two-thirds of the state in low, moist, open or shaded sites.

USE. Gaping panicum is a succulent, early-growing and early-flowering native perennial that provides a fair amount of forage in low pastures along swale areas and on borders of streams and lakes.

104. Vinemesquite *Panicum obtusum* H.B.K.
Perennial with erect, leafy stems and long, wiry stolons from a hard, knotty or rhizomatous base, often forming large colonies or mats. *Stems* mostly 20–60 cm tall, the erect stems with hairless nodes. *Stolons* to 1 m or more in length, with swollen, densely hairy nodes. *Sheaths* rounded, hairless or bristly, the reduced basal leaves usually densely soft-haired. *Blades* firm, elongate, flat or inrolled, 2–7 mm broad, light bluish green, usually with a few long hairs above the ligule, but otherwise hairless. *Inflorescence* a narrow, contracted panicle or raceme mostly 3–10 cm long and 5–13 mm broad, with short, closely appressed, usually unbranched primary branches, or with spikelets all short-stalked on the main axis. *Spikelets* oblong or obovate, 3.4–4 mm long, hairless. *Glumes* broad, rounded at the tip, nearly equal and as long as the spikelet or slightly shorter. *Lower floret* usually with stamens only, with a large, well-developed palea that often exceeds the lemma in length. *Lemma of upper (seed-bearing) floret* shiny, minutely pitted. Plants setting seed May to October.

Fig. 103.   Gaping panicum *(Panicum hians)* plant and spikelet.

172 : Common Texas Grasses

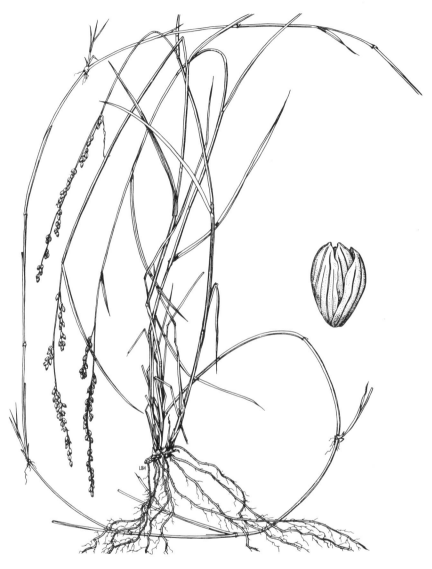

Fig. 104. Vinemesquite *(Panicum obtusum)* plant and spikelet.

DISTRIBUTION AND HABITAT. Vinemesquite grows throughout the state except in the Pineywoods. It occurs mostly in clayey lowland pastures, swales, and ditches that periodically dry out.

USE. This species is a native, warm-season perennial that provides good grazing for livestock and fair grazing for wildlife.

105. Switchgrass *Panicum virgatum* L.

Stout perennial with scaly, creeping rhizomes and firm, tough stems 0.6–2 m or up to 3 m tall, in large or small clumps, usually unbranched above the base. *Stem nodes* hairless or hairy. *Sheaths* rounded, hairless. *Blades* firm, flat, elongate, 3–15 mm broad, commonly hairless but occasionally with soft, straight hairs. *Panicles* open, broad or rather narrow, many-flowered, 15–55 cm long, with spikelets mostly short-stalked and clustered on long, slender branches. *Spikelets* hairless, 3–5 mm long. *Glumes* narrowly pointed, the first two-thirds to three-fourths as long as the second, the second as long as the spikelet. *Lower floret* usually with stamens only and with a large, thin palea. *Lemma of upper (seed-bearing) floret* narrowly ovate, smooth and shiny, light-colored. Plants setting seed late August to October.

DISTRIBUTION AND HABITAT. Switchgrass grows nearly throughout the state in moist lowlands on sandy or clayey soils.

USE. A native, cool-season perennial bunch grass that provides good grazing for livestock and fair grazing for wildlife, switchgrass has developed a number of ecotypes, some of which are quite different from the common lowland bunch grass. Several commercial selections of switchgrass for range reseeding are offered by seed dealers.

PAPPOPHORUM

106. Pink pappusgrass *Pappophorum bicolor* Fourn.

Perennial bunch grass with stems stiffly erect or somewhat abruptly bent, mostly 30–80 cm tall. *Sheaths* with a tuft of long hairs on either side of the collar, the hairs falling in age. *Blades* flat or inrolled, rough on the upper surface above their base, smooth on the lower surface, mostly 10–20 cm long and 1.5–5 mm broad. *Panicle* tightly or loosely contracted, with short, erect or spreading branches, pink- or purple-tinged at maturity, mostly 12–20 cm long. *Spikelets* short-stalked, closely pressed against the branchlets, 6–8 mm long, with two or three seed-bearing florets and two reduced florets above. *Glumes* broad, hairless, pointed or minutely notched and with a small, short, abrupt tip, usually 3–4 mm long. *Lemmas* broad, firm, rounded, many-nerved, hairy on the midnerve and margins from the base to the middle, dissected at the tip into eleven to fifteen awns of irregular lengths, the longest 2.5–5 mm long. *Body of lower lemmas* 3–4 mm long. *Rudimentary upper florets* similar to the seed-bearing ones but smaller. Plants setting seed April to November.

DISTRIBUTION AND HABITAT. Pink pappusgrass is found in southern, central, and western Texas on grassy plains, on moist road rights-of-way, and in open valleys.

USE. This grass is a native, warm-season perennial that provides fair grazing for livestock and poor grazing for wildlife.

Fig. 105.   Switchgrass *(Panicum virgatum)* inflorescence, floret, and spikelet.

Fig. 106.   Pink pappusgrass *(Pappophorum bicolor)* inflorescence, spikelet, and floret.

176 : Common Texas Grasses

PASPALIDIUM

107. Egyptian paspalidium *Paspalidium geminatum* (Forsk.) Stapf

Perennial with stems in small clumps from a firm base often forming rhizomes. *Stems and leaves* hairless. *Blades* linear, 3–6 mm broad, flat or folded. *Inflorescence* a narrow, elongate panicle with spikelets short-stalked on seven to seventeen short, spikelike branches. *Inflorescence branches* single at the nodes, widely spaced below and progressively closer together above. *Spikelets* borne singly in two rows on the flattened branch main axis, oriented with the rounded back of the lemma of the upper (seed-bearing) floret turned towards the main axis as in *Paspalum* species. *Spikelets* breaking off below the glumes, 2.2–3 mm long, ovate or elliptic, hairless, two-flowered, the lower floret neuter or with stamens only and the upper seed-bearing. *First glume* broad, rounded or truncate, one-fourth to one-third as long as the spikelet. *Palea of lower floret* well developed, about as long as the lemma. *Lemma of upper floret* finely roughened, pointed at the tip. Plants setting seed April to September.

DISTRIBUTION AND HABITAT. Egyptian paspalidium grows in the eastern and southern portions of the state, mostly along streams, lakes, and ditches and often in standing water.

USE. This species is a grass of marshy pastures and shores of ponds and lakes. It is of fair forage value for livestock and wildlife, but it seldom grows in large stands.

PASPALUM

Key to the species:

Inflorescence branches two (occasionally three), paired or less than 1 cm apart .... Bahiagrass, *P. notatum*

Inflorescence branches one to numerous; when two, then the branches 1–2 cm or more apart

  Margins of spikelets fringed with long hairs

    Inflorescence branches mostly three to six ....
    .... Dallisgrass, *P. dilatatum*

    Inflorescence branches mostly twelve to twenty ....
    .... Vaseygrass, *P. urvillei*

  Margins of spikelets not fringed with long hairs

    First glume present on some or all spikelets ....
    .... Gulfdune paspalum, *P. monostachyum*

    First glume absent on all spikelets

      Grain dark brown and shiny at maturity, wrinkled on the flat side .... Brownseed paspalum, *P. plicatulum*

      Grain green, light brown, or straw-colored at maturity

        Spikelets 1.5–2.6 mm long

Fig. 107.   Egyptian paspalidium *(Paspalidium geminatum)* inflorescence and spikelet.

178 : Common Texas Grasses

Spikelets elliptic or obovate; plants usually with long, creeping stolons .... Longtom, *P. lividum*
Spikelets nearly orbicular, broadly ovate or broadly obovate; plants without long, creeping stolons ....
.... Thin paspalum, *P. setaceum*
Spikelets 3–4.8 mm long .... *P. floridanum*

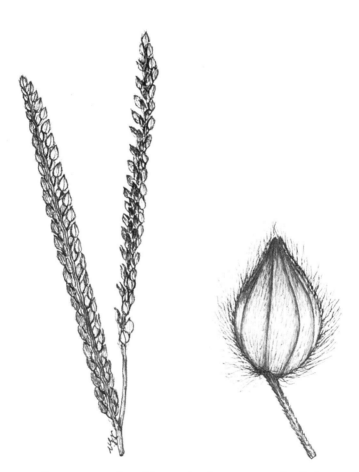

Fig. 108.   Dallisgrass *(Paspalum dilatatum)* inflorescence and spikelet.

108. Dallisgrass   *Paspalum dilatatum* Poir.

Perennial bunch grass with stems mostly 50–120 cm tall from a hard, knotty base. *Lowermost sheaths* usually hairy, the upper sheaths hairless. *Blades* firm, flat, tapering to a narrow point, mostly 3–12 mm broad, hairless or sparsely fringed with long hairs near the base. *Inflorescence branches* mostly two to seven, usually widely spaced on a slender central axis. *Spikelets* closely overlapped in four rows on a broad, flat branch 3–8 cm long. *Spikelets* broadly ovate, tapering to a short point. *First glume* absent, the second glume and lemma of lower floret with three to five nerves, 3–4 mm long, downy on the margins with long, silky hairs. *Lemma of upper (seed-bearing) floret* light-colored, broadly ovate or nearly orbicular. Plants setting seed April to November.

DISTRIBUTION AND HABITAT. Dallisgrass occurs throughout the state except on the High Plains and Rolling Plains. It is seeded as a forage grass and persists in pastures and as a weed of roadsides, lawns, and waste places in the southern part of the state.

USE. Dallisgrass is an introduced, warm-season perennial native to Uruguay and Argentina. It provides good grazing for livestock and fair grazing for wildlife. Under proper management it makes good stands in bottomland pastures.

109. *Paspalum floridanum* Michx.
Key to the varieties:
Leaves more or less densely hairy ....
.... Florida paspalum, *P. floridanum* var. *floridanum*
Leaves hairless or nearly so except in the vicinity of the ligule ....
.... Bald Florida paspalum, *P. floridanum* var. *glabratum*

109a. Florida paspalum *Paspalum floridanum* Michx. var. *floridanum*
Stems stout, 1–2 m tall, from short, thick rhizomes. *Sheaths and blades*, at least in part, densely hairy. *Blades* firm, flat or folded, mostly 4–10 mm broad and to as much as 50 cm long, with a dense tuft of long hairs immediately above the ligule. *Inflorescence* usually with two to five branches, these 4–13 cm long. *Spikelets* hairless, broadly elliptic to suborbicular, 3.6–4.8 mm long, short-stalked in pairs and closely placed in four rows on the branch axis. *Lemma of lower floret* with a well-developed midnerve. *Lemma of upper (seed-bearing) floret* light brown, minutely roughened. Plants bearing seed mostly August to November.

DISTRIBUTION AND HABITAT. Florida paspalum grows in the eastern part of Texas, mostly in low, moist pastures, openings in woods, and cut-over woodlands. It is much less frequent in Texas than the bald Florida paspalum (var. *glabratum*).

USE. This native, warm-season perennial is a fair forage grass for livestock and a poor forage grass for wildlife.

109b. Bald Florida paspalum *Paspalum floridanum* Michx. var. *glabratum* Engelm. *ex* Vasey
Similar to var. *floridanum*, but the sheaths and blades nearly or

Fig. 109b.   Bald Florida paspalum (*Paspalum floridanum* var. *glabratum*) plant, spikelet, and floret.

completely hairless. On many specimens the blade is conspicuously hairy immediately above the ligule, but otherwise hairless.

DISTRIBUTION AND HABITAT. Bald Florida paspalum is widespread and frequent in grasslands and open woodlands throughout eastern and central Texas, but it is never locally abundant.

USE. This variety is a native, warm-season perennial of fair forage value for livestock and of poor forage value for wildlife.

110. Longtom *Paspalum lividum* Trin.

Perennial with stems mostly 30–70 cm tall curving upward from a spreading base that forms stolons often 1 m or more in length. *Stems* flattened, usually with many nodes and short internodes. *Sheaths* thin, hairless, or bristly with swollen-based hairs, the lower ones sharply keeled, gradually tapering to a narrow apex, soon withering or broken off and exposing the numerous dark-colored stem nodes. *Blades* mostly 3–6 mm broad, hairless or the surface on the side toward the stem sparsely hairy. *Inflorescence* of usually three to seven short, simple, spreading or erect branches, these mostly 1.5–4 mm long. *Branch axis* 1.5–2 mm wide, with or without a few scattered long hairs, often becoming dark purple. *Spikelets* closely overlapped in four rows on the branch axis, 2–2.5 mm long, hairless, elliptic or obovate, broadly pointed. *Glume and lemma of lower floret* thin and papery at maturity. *Lemma and palea of upper (seed-bearing) floret* finely roughened, straw-colored. Plants setting seed May to October.

DISTRIBUTION AND HABITAT. Longtom grows in eastern Texas and along the coastal plain in ditches, in swales, and along muddy coastal flats.

USE. This native, warm-season perennial is rated good for livestock grazing and fair for wildlife grazing.

111. Gulfdune paspalum *Paspalum monostachyum* Vasey

Stout perennial with stems 50–120 cm tall arising singly or in small clusters from long, stout, scaly rhizomes. *Leaves* hairless except for the long-fringed ligule. *Blades* long and linear, inrolled, 2 mm or less in width (as inrolled), the lower ones mostly 20–30 cm or more long. *Inflorescence branches* spikelike, one to three or four, mostly 10–25 cm long. *Spikelets* hairless, broadly elliptic, 3–3.5 mm long, usually in pairs of one short-stalked and one long-stalked, but the long stalk occasionally replaced by a short branch bearing three to six crowded spikelets. *First glume* absent or irregularly developed on some spikelets. *Lemma of lower floret* straw-colored or light brown. Plants setting seed May to November.

DISTRIBUTION AND HABITAT. Gulfdune paspalum occurs along the Gulf Coast in sandy soils, most frequently on coastal dune formations.

USE. This grass is of only fair forage value for livestock and wildlife, producing little herbage.

Fig. 110. Longtom *(Paspalum lividum)* plant and spikelet.

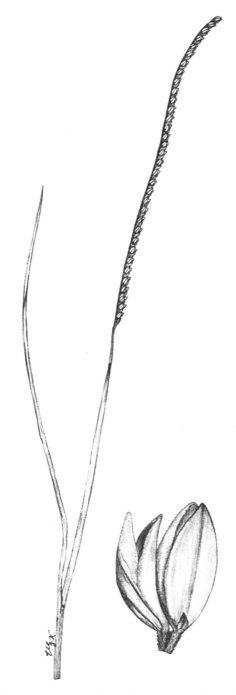

Fig. 111. Gulfdune paspalum *(Paspalum monostachyum)* inflorescence and spikelet pair.

112. Bahiagrass *Paspalum notatum* Flugge

Perennial bunch grass with erect stems mostly 20–75 cm tall. Plants often developing thick, scaly rhizomes. *Leaves* hairless or essentially so. *Blades* 2–6 mm broad, flat, folded, or inrolled, usually firm and tough in texture. *Inflorescence* typically with two spikelike branches 4–12 cm long, these paired at the tip of the stem or with one slightly below the other, and a third branch infrequently present below the terminal ones. *Spikelets* closely overlapping in two rows, broad and rounded, hairless and shiny, 2.8–3.5 mm long. *Lemma of upper (seed-bearing) floret* straw-colored. Plants setting seed June to November.

DISTRIBUTION AND HABITAT. Bahiagrass is found along the coastal plain, where it is grown as a pasture grass and for soil stabilization. It is occasional on roadsides, along ditches, and in other slightly disturbed sites with adequate moisture.

USE. Bahiagrass is a warm-season, introduced perennial grown rather extensively for forage and for erosion control in the eastern and southeastern United States. It has rather fibrous herbage when mature, providing only fair forage for livestock and poor forage for wildlife. One of the introduced strains or varieties of Bahiagrass that has been reported from Texas bears the name *P. notatum* var. *saurae* Parodi. This variety is a large, coarse plant with long blades and small spikelets (3 mm or less long).

113. Brownseed paspalum *Paspalum plicatulum* Michx.

Perennial bunch grass with stems 50–100 cm tall in small or moderately large clumps from firm, stout, often rhizomatous bases. *Stems* slender, stiffly erect, hairless or the lower nodes downy. *Sheaths* keeled, without hairs or less frequently hairy. *Blades* firm, folded at their base, mostly 3–7 mm broad, hairless or more commonly with thick-based, soft, straight hairs on the upper surface near the base. *Inflorescence branches* simple and spikelike, usually three to ten, commonly 3–10 cm long and with pairs of unequally stalked spikelets closely crowded on either side of the flattened branch axis. *Spikelets* dark brown, broadly elliptic or obovate, 2.4–2.8 mm long. *Glume* hairless or with minute, closely appressed down. *Lemma of lower floret* thin, usually with wrinkles across the margins. *Lemma of upper (seed-bearing) floret* dark brown and shiny, minutely roughened. Plants setting seed nearly throughout the year but flowering mainly May to November.

DISTRIBUTION AND HABITAT. Brownseed paspalum is found throughout the eastern and central regions of the state, most frequently on rather sandy sterile or sandy loam soils, often in partial shade in open oak woodlands.

USE. This bunch grass is a native, warm-season perennial providing fair grazing for livestock and wildlife.

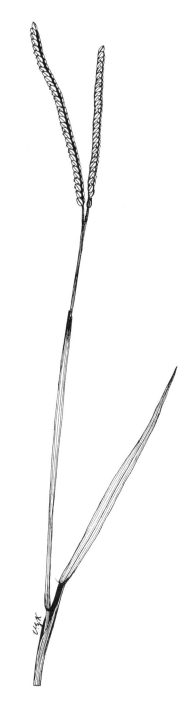

Fig. 112.   Bahiagrass *(Paspalum notatum)* inflorescence.

186 : Common Texas Grasses

Fig. 113.   Brownseed paspalum *(Paspalum plicatulum)* inflorescence and pair of spikelets.

Fig. 114. Thin paspalum *(Paspalum setaceum)* inflorescence and spikelet.

114. Thin paspalum *Paspalum setaceum* Michx.

Tufted, short-lived perennial with stems mostly 30–80 cm tall from a knotty base or from short rhizomes. *Blades* flat, variable in length, 2–20 mm broad, hairless or variously hairy, soft or rather firm, with long, silvery hairs just above the ligule. *Inflorescences* commonly borne both at the tip of the main stem and in the axils of the upper leaves, the spikelets in a single spikelike raceme or in a panicle of two to five spikelike branches. *Inflorescence branches* slender, 3–17 cm long. *Lateral inflorescences* often partially hidden in the leaf sheaths. *Spikelets* broadly elliptic to orbicular, 1.4–2.6 mm long, hairless or downy. Plants setting seed mainly May to October.

Several populations of widely variable but intergrading plant types of this warm-season perennial are included in this species. In *The Grasses of Texas* (Gould, 1975) five varieties are recognized.

DISTRIBUTION AND HABITAT. Thin paspalum is present in all regions of Texas, but it is most common in the eastern half of the state, growing on both sandy and clayey soils, most frequently in heavily grazed pastures, ditches, and borders of woods.

USE. Thin paspalum is a native, warm-season perennial with several rather distinct types recognized as varieties. These grasses provide fair forage for livestock and wildlife but usually occupy a low position in plant succession on rangelands.

115. Vaseygrass *Paspalum urvillei* Steud.

Coarse perennial with stiffly erect stems mostly 1–2 m tall, usually in large, leafy clumps. *Base of plant* firm or hard. *Lower sheaths* usually hairy with long hairs, the upper sheaths without hairs. *Blades* long and coarse, mostly 4–15 mm broad, usually hairless except for a tuft of hair immediately above the ligule. *Inflorescence* a panicle with usually eight to thirty closely placed, erect branches, these mostly 4–10 cm long. *Spikelets* closely spaced and overlapping in four rows, 2.2–2.7 mm long, hairy on the back and margins, ovate to obovate, abruptly pointed. *First glume* absent. *Second glume and lemma of lower floret* downy with long hairs on the margins, the lemma also downy on the back. *Lemma of upper (seed-bearing) floret* light-colored. Plants setting seed May to November.

DISTRIBUTION AND HABITAT. Vaseygrass grows in the eastern and central parts of the state, usually along lakes, swales, ditches, and low moist areas. It is frequent as a weed of roadside ditches.

USE. An introduced perennial from South America that has become common and somewhat weedy on disturbed soils in the southern United States, Vaseygrass tends to be coarse and fibrous, and it is only a fair forage plant for livestock.

Fig. 115. Vaseygrass *(Paspalum urvillei)* plant, two views of spikelet, and floret.

PHALARIS

116. Carolina canarygrass *Phalaris caroliniana* Walt.

Tufted annual with weak, hollow stems mostly 25–70 cm tall. *Leaves* hairless. *Ligule* membranous, 3–5 mm long. *Blades* soft, flat, 6–15 cm long and 3–10 mm broad. *Panicle* tightly contracted, cylindrical, 3–8 cm

Fig. 116.   Carolina canarygrass *(Phalaris caroliniana)* plant, spikelet, and floret.

long and 8–13 mm broad. *Spikelets* awnless, with one terminal seed-bearing floret and one or two rudimentary, scalelike florets below. *Glumes* large, broad, about equal, longer than the seed-bearing floret, mostly 5–6 mm long, the keel with a greenish wing. *Lemma of seed-bearing floret* shiny, ovate to lanceolate, 3–4 mm long, with closely pressed whitish hairs. *Reduced florets* narrow, scalelike, somewhat unequal, one-third to one-half as long as the lemma of the seed-bearing floret and closely placed at its base. *Grain* 1.7–2 mm long, oblong, brownish. Plants setting seed March to June.

DISTRIBUTION AND HABITAT. Carolina canarygrass grows in all regions of Texas in grasslands and in open woodlands. It is especially abundant in disturbed soils along roadsides, on stream and ditch banks, and along fence rows.

USE. A native, cool-season, short-lived annual of essentially no value as a forage plant, Carolina canarygrass is closely related to the canarygrass of commerce *(Phalaris canariensis)*, a common constituent of birdseed.

PHRAGMITES

117. Common reed   *Phragmites australis* (Cav.) Trin. *ex* Steud.

Stout, tall perennial with stems 2–4 m tall from thick, creeping rhizomes. *Blades* flat, elongate, minutely roughened on the margins, those of the main stems mostly 1.5–5 cm broad. *Panicle* densely flowered and contracted, with spikelets borne on slender, closely appressed stalks and branchlets. *Spikelets* 10–15 mm long, mostly with four to eight florets. *Joints of spikelet axis* densely hairy, the hairs 1 cm or more long. *Glumes, lemmas and paleas* thin, hairless. *First glume* one-half to two-thirds as long as the second, three-nerved. *Second glume* with three to five nerves, mostly 6–8 mm long, pointed. *Lower floret* infertile, with a three-nerved, narrowly pointed lemma mostly 11–14 mm long, much longer than the lemmas of the upper florets. Plants setting seed mostly July to November.

DISTRIBUTION AND HABITAT. Common reed is occasional throughout the state, but it is most frequent along the coast, along the borders of streams and lakes, and in marshes, often in standing water.

USE. This tall grass is a native, warm-season perennial of little or no value as a forage grass but providing habitat and grain for all kinds of birds.

POA

Key to the species:
Plants annual; lemmas soft-haired . . . . Annual bluegrass, *P. annua*

Fig. 117.   Common reed *(Phragmites australis)* inflorescence and spikelet.

Plants perennial; lemmas hairy or hairless
    Plants with either male (with anthers) or female (with pistils) spikelets;
        panicles narrow, densely flowered . . . .
        . . . . Texas bluegrass, *P. arachnifera*
    Plants with bisexual spikelets; panicles open, not dense . . . .
        . . . . Kentucky bluegrass, *P. pratensis*

Accounts of the Grasses : 193

118. Annual bluegrass *Poa annua* L.

Tufted annual with weak, spreading stems mostly 6–30 cm long. *Leaves* hairless, bright green. *Blades* thin, flat, mostly 1.5–4 mm broad and 2–12 mm long. *Panicles* typically open, well projecting above or hidden in the basal tuft of leaves, mostly 3–8 cm long, the lower branches tending to be stiffly spreading and bare of spikelets on the lower one-third to one-half. *Glumes* thin, broad, slightly unequal, the first with one to three nerves and the second with three nerves. *Lemmas* broad, with papery margins, 3–3.5 mm long, with equally developed nerves, variously downy to nearly hairless, the hairs commonly on the midnerve and marginal nerves but occasional on the intermediate nerves. *Basal tuft* of long, kinky hairs not developed on the lemmas. Plants setting seed November to May.

DISTRIBUTION AND HABITAT. Annual bluegrass is grown throughout the state, mostly in watered or irrigated areas such as lawns, parks, golf courses, and irrigated pastures. It was originally introduced from Europe and is now established as a casual or weedy grass throughout the United States.

USE. Annual bluegrass is of no significance as a forage grass. It usually is the first cool-season grass to flower in the fall and winter.

119. Texas bluegrass *Poa arachnifera* Torr.

Tufted perennial with long, slender rhizomes. *Stems* stiffly erect, 35–50 cm tall, often densely clustered. *Leaves* hairless. *Blades* elongate, flat or less frequently inrolled, 1–5 mm broad. *Male and female spikelets* on separate plants in contracted, narrow, sometimes lobed panicles mostly 5–15 cm long, with lower branches 2–7 cm long. *Lowermost node of panicle* usually with two to four branches, these spikelet-bearing to their base or bare of spikelets on the lower half. *Spikelets* large, with three to eight florets. *Female spikelets* densely woolly with down, with long, kinky hairs attached at the base of the lemma or on the spikelet axis joints immediately below the lemma. *Male spikelets* not conspicuously hairy, but usually with a few long, kinky hairs at the base of the florets. *Glumes and lemmas* broad, thin, papery, pointed. *Lemmas of female spikelets* mostly 5–6 mm long. *Lemmas of male spikelets* 3–5 mm long. Plants setting seed May to June.

DISTRIBUTION AND HABITAT. Texas bluegrass is occasional throughout the state except in the far west. It grows in prairies and along the edges of woods bordering prairie sites.

USE. This grass is a native, cool-season perennial providing good grazing for livestock and fair grazing for wildlife.

Fig. 118.   Annual bluegrass *(Poa annua)* plant and spikelet.

Fig. 119.   Texas bluegrass *(Poa arachnifera). Center:* panicle of female (pistillate)
spikelets; *below:* female spikelet and floret; *above:* male (staminate) spikelet and
floret.

196 : Common Texas Grasses

120. Kentucky bluegrass *Poa pratensis* L.

Perennial with slender, widely spreading rhizomes. *Stems* relatively slender and wiry, mostly 20–80 cm tall, mostly curving erect from individual, prostrate, rhizomatous bases. *Sheaths* hairless, the blades firm, flat, 1–4 mm broad, usually short and dull green. *Panicles* mostly 5–10 cm long and 3–5 cm broad, typically open, with slender, flexuous branches, at least the lower ones spreading. *Branches at lowermost node of main axis* mostly four to six, bare of spikelets on lower one-half to two-thirds. *Spikelets* 3–6 mm long, with three to six flowers. *Glumes* broad, usually strongly keeled, slightly unequal in length. *Lemmas* usually hairy on midnerve and margins, the intermediate nerves hairless, the base with a tuft of long, silky hairs. Plants setting seed in Texas April to June.

DISTRIBUTION AND HABITAT. Kentucky bluegrass is occasional in the northern and western portions of Texas, mostly occuring as a weed of fields, gardens, and other disturbed sites. It is native to the Old World and possibly to the northern mountainous areas of North America.

USE. This grass is an introduced, cool-season perennial providing good forage for livestock in many areas of the United States but in Texas occurring mainly as a weed of disturbed soils. Selections of Kentucky bluegrass have been developed into fine lawn grasses, but they are of most value in the cooler regions of the country.

POLYPOGON

121. Rabbitfootgrass *Polypogon monspeliensis* (L.) Desf.

Tufted annual with weak stems usually curving erect, 8–70 cm tall, often rooting at the lower nodes. *Ligules* with many nerves, 4–10 mm long. *Blades* flat, rough on one or both surfaces, mostly 2–8 mm broad. *Inflorescence* a dense, contracted panicle, bristly with yellowish awns, often lobed but seldom interrupted, 2–15 cm or more long, 1–2.5 cm broad. *Spikelets* single-flowered, short-stalked, and densely congested on short branches. *Glumes* about equal, thin, narrow, short-haired, usually minutely lobed at the tip. *Lemmas and paleas* translucent, much shorter than the glumes, the lemma usually with a delicate deciduous awn about 1 mm long. *Grains* minutely roughened, brownish, 1 mm or less long. Plants setting seed mostly March to July.

DISTRIBUTION AND HABITAT. Rabbitfootgrass is occasional throughout the state along streams, in swales, in moist ditches, and in waste places, usually in sandy soils. It is a European species now widespread in North America.

USE. This grass is an introduced, cool-season annual of no significance as a forage grass.

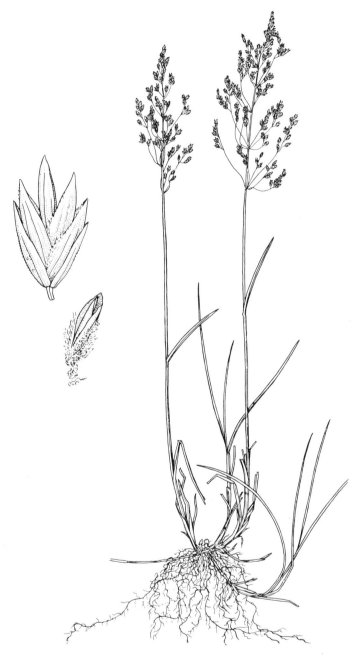

Fig. 120.   Kentucky bluegrass *(Poa pratensis)* plant, spikelet, and floret.

Fig. 121. Rabbitfootgrass (*Polypogon monspeliensis*) plant, spikelet, and floret.

Fig. 122. Tumblegrass *(Schedonnardus paniculatus)* inflorescence and spikelet.

SCHEDONNARDUS

122. Tumblegrass *Schedonnardus paniculatus* (Nutt.) Trel.

Low, tufted perennial with slender, stiff stems curving erect. *Stems* slender, wiry, mostly 8–50 cm long, often curving upward from a spreading base. *Leaves* hairless. *Sheaths* laterally compressed and keeled, with broad, translucent margins that are continued at the apex as a membranous, rounded ligule mostly 1–3 mm long. *Blades* 2–12 cm long and 0.6–2.5 mm broad, rough on the margins, often folded on the strong midnerve and spirally twisted when dried. *Panicles* with a curved main axis equaling or much longer than the leafy portion of the stem, with few widely spaced, spikelike branches. Panicle eventually breaking off at the base and rolling as a tumbleweed. *Spikelets* slender, unstalked, 3–4 mm long, widely spaced and closely pressed against the branches and the upper part of the panicle axis, breaking off above the glumes as well as at the base of the inflorescence. *Glumes* narrow, narrowly pointed, single-nerved, the second about as long as the lemma and the first shorter. *Lemmas* narrow, rigid, three-nerved, narrowly pointed or with a minute awn tip, hairless. *Grain* narrow, 2.5–3.5 mm long. Plants setting seed throughout the year under favorable conditions of growth.

DISTRIBUTION AND HABITAT. Tumblegrass grows throughout the state, most frequently on clay or clay loam soils.

USE. This species is a native, warm-season perennial grass of range-lands that develops little herbage and has little value for livestock or wildlife grazing.

SCHIZACHYRIUM

123. *Schizachyrium scoparium* (Michx.) Nash

Perennial bunch grass with stiffly erect stems 50–200 cm tall. *Stems* green or with a whitish waxy coating, freely branching above to produce numerous flowering branches. *Sheaths* strongly keeled and laterally flattened, up to 10 mm broad on some plants, but usually much narrower, hairless or with long, soft, unmatted hairs. *Blades* linear and long-tapered at the tip, the basal ones mostly 1.5–4 mm broad and 25 cm or more long, hairless or sparsely hairy. *Inflorescence* a slender raceme. *Spikelets* in pairs of one stalkless and one stalked on an unbranched central axis. *Racemes* often numerous and clustered on the much-branched flowering stem, mostly 2.5–5 cm long, each subtended by a sheath. *Raceme axis joints and spikelet stalks* fringed with long, silvery hairs, at least on the upper two-thirds. *Stalkless spikelets* mostly 6–8 mm long, the first glume hairless or with prickle-hairs, the lemma 8–15 mm long. *Stalked spikelets* with stamens only or neuter, as large as stalkless ones to much smaller, awnless or with a short, straight awn. Plants setting seed August to December.

Key to the varieties:
Lower sheaths and blades densely hairy with long, soft hairs; occurring in
    southeastern Texas . . . .
    . . . . Eastern little bluestem, S. *scoparium* var. *divergens*
Lower sheaths and blades hairless or sparsely hairy
    Plants not developing rhizomes; stems and sheaths moderately com-
        pressed, the sheaths weakly or strongly keeled . . . .
        . . . . Little bluestem, S. *scoparium* var. *frequens*

Fig. 123b.   Little bluestem (*Schizachyrium scoparium* var. *frequens*) plant and spikelet pair.

Plants developing rhizomes; stems and sheaths strongly compressed and sharply keeled; inflorescence axis joints and spikelet stalks more or less densely haired with long, soft hairs; occurring in southeastern and southern Texas ....
.... Seacoast bluestem, *S. scoparium* var. *littoralis*

123a. Eastern little bluestem *Schizachyrium scoparium* var. *divergens* (Hack.) Gould

Plants not producing rhizomes. *Sheaths and blades* at least in part with long, shaggy, unmatted hairs. *Stalked spikelets* with two large, well-developed glumes, these often as long as those of the stalkless spikelets.

DISTRIBUTION AND HABITAT. This grass, found in eastern Texas, is a shade-tolerant variety of little bluestem that is frequent in open pine forests and pine-hardwood woodlands.

USE. Eastern little bluestem is a native, warm-season perennial that provides good forage for livestock and for wildlife.

In eastern Texas, plants of this variety (var. *divergens*) frequently grow interminged with little bluestem (var. *frequens*) and with another *S. scoparium* variety, var. *virile* Shinners, which has relatively large, well-developed stalked spikelets. All of the varieties of little bluestem are similar in vegetative characteristics and forage value.

123b. Little bluestem *Schizachyrium scoparium* var. *frequens* (C. E. Hubb.) Gould

Plants not developing creeping rhizomes. *Leaves* hairless or sparsely hairy. *Inflorescence axis and spikelet stalks* hairy but not densely longhaired. *Stalked spikelets* narrower and shorter than the unstalked ones.

DISTRIBUTION AND HABITAT. Found throughout the state except in the Pineywoods, little bluestem is a dominant of the tall-grass prairies and is frequent on well-managed open rangeland, on rocky slopes, and in openings in woods.

USE. This grass is a native, warm-season perennial that provides good grazing for all types of livestock and wildlife. The presence of vigorous stands of little bluestem on a range is a general indication of good land and good management.

123c. Seacoast bluestem *Schizachyrium scoparium* var. *littoralis* (Nash) Gould

Plants with well-developed rhizomes and strongly compressed and keeled sheaths. Herbage with a whitish waxy coating. *Inflorescence joints and spikelet stalks* densely hairy.

DISTRIBUTION AND HABITAT. Seacoast bluestem occurs along the coast and in southern Texas, typically in deep sand and commonly on coastal sands near sea level in southern Texas. In the southern part of the range, seacoast bluestem occasionally may flower as early as June.

USE. This variety is a good forage grass for both livestock and deer.

SCLEROPOGON

124. Burrograss *Scleropogon brevifolius* Phil.

Low sod-forming perennial with male and female spikelets on separate plants and often in more or less separate colonies. *Flowering stems* tufted, erect, mostly 10–25 cm tall from wiry creeping stolons. *Leaves* mainly in a basal cluster. *Sheaths* short, strongly nerved, the upper sheaths hairless but those at the base of the plant often hairy. *Blades* firm, flat or folded, 1–2 mm broad and mostly 2–8 cm long. *Spikelets* large, in few-flowered spikelike racemes or contracted panicles, the male spikelets (with stamens only) awnless, the female spikelets (with pistil only) long-awned. *Male (staminate) spikelets* with five to ten, and occasionally up to twenty, florets. *Glumes and lemmas of male spikelets* similar, thin, pale, lanceolate, usually three-nerved. *Female (pistillate) spikelets* mostly with three to five fertile florets and one or several awnlike rudimentary florets above, the florets breaking off together. *Glumes of female spikelets* unequal, lanceolate, awnless, three-nerved, occasionally with additional fine lateral nerves. *Lemmas of female spikelets* firm, rounded on the back, three-nerved, the nerves extending into stout awns 5–10 cm long. *Paleas* narrow, the two nerves short-awned. Plants setting seed mostly in late summer, but occasionally also in the spring.

DISTRIBUTION AND HABITAT. Burrograss grows in the central and western portions of the state on open, dry, rocky slopes and plains.

USE. A native, warm-season perennial of low palatability and of little value as a forage plant, burrograss often develops large, dense stands and apparently spreads in heavily grazed areas.

SETARIA

Key to the species:
Bristles of inflorescence usually present only at the base of the terminal
    spikelet of each branchlet as an extension of the branchlet axis . . . . . .
    . . . . Reverchon bristlegrass, *S. reverchonii*
Bristles present below all or nearly all spikelets
  Bristles four to twelve below each spikelet; lemma of upper floret
    coarsely roughened transversely . . . .
    . . . . Knotroot bristlegrass, *S. geniculata*
  Bristles one to three below each spikelet; lemma of upper floret finely
    roughened . . . . Plains bristlegrass, *S. leucopila*

Fig. 124.   Burrograss (*Scleropogon brevifolius*) male (staminate) plant, awnless
male spikelet, and awned female (pistillate) spikelet.

Fig. 125.   Knotroot bristlegrass *(Setaria geniculata)* inflorescence and spikelet.

125. Knotroot bristlegrass   *Setaria geniculata* (Lam.) Beauv.

Perennial with tufted stems 30–80 cm tall from short, knotty rhizomes. *Nodes* hairless. *Leaves* typically hairless but occasionally with long hairs in the vicinity of the ligule. *Sheaths*, at least the lower ones, usually keeled. *Blades* flat, 2–8 mm broad, mostly 6–25 cm long. *Panicles* densely flowered, contracted and cylindrical, mostly 3–8 cm long. *Panicle axis* minutely hairy, hidden by the spikelets. *Bristles* four to twelve below each spikelet, rough (with short prickle-hairs), yellow, tawny, green, or purple in color, variable in length, but mostly 5–10 mm long. *Spikelets* 2.5–3 mm long, elliptical, plump. *Glumes* thin, shorter than the spikelet, the first about one-third as long and the second two-thirds to three-fourths as long. *Lemma of lower floret* about as long as the lemma of the upper floret. *Lemma of upper floret* hard, coarsely roughened crosswise, pointed or slightly beaked at the tip. Plants setting seed almost throughout the year under favorable conditions.

DISTRIBUTION AND HABITAT. Knotroot bristlegrass is reported from all regions of the state and is one of the most common grasses in moist habitats along streams, ditches, and borders of lakes and ponds.

USE. This species is a native, warm-season perennial that provides fair grazing for livestock and wildlife.

126. Plains bristlegrass   *Setaria leucopila* (Scribn. & Merr.) K. Schum.
Strong perennial with stiffly erect stems mostly 26–100 cm tall. *Herbage* usually pale or with a whitish waxy coating. *Stems* in dense clumps, infrequently branched, rough and often somewhat hairy below the nodes. *Sheaths* long-haired along the upper margins. *Blades* flat or folded, 8–25 cm long, typically 2–5 mm broad but occasionally broader, hairless or infrequently hairy. *Inflorescence* a densely flowered, contracted panicle, commonly 6–15 cm long but shorter in some forms, 0.7–1.5 cm thick. *Panicle axis* rough and more or less hairy. *Bristles* 4–15 mm long, usually solitary below each spikelet. *Spikelets* 2.1–2.7 mm long at maturity. *Palea of lower floret* one-half to three-fourths as long as the lemma of the lower floret. *Lemma and palea of upper floret* finely roughened and with cross-wrinkles, the paleas flat or slightly rounded. Plants setting seed May to November.

DISTRIBUTION AND HABITAT. Plains bristlegrass grows throughout the drier portions of the state and is absent from the Blackland Prairie, Post Oak Savanna, and Pineywoods of eastern Texas.

USE. An important native, warm-season perennial that provides good grazing for livestock and fair grazing for wildlife, plains bristlegrass usually does not occur in large stands but is frequent throughout its areas of distribution. It is well adapted to open, dry sites and is most frequent on well-drained soils along gulleys, stream courses, and other areas with occasional abundant moisture. Plains bristlegrass is a good grass to include in a mixture for seeding after mechanical brush control.

127. Reverchon bristlegrass   *Setaria reverchonii* (Vasey) Pilger
Tufted perennial with stiffly erect stems mostly 35–70 cm tall from a hard, often somewhat rhizomatous base. *Scale leaves* at base of plant usually densely hairy, the lower sheaths also more or less hairy, at least on

Fig. 126.   Plains bristlegrass *(Setaria leucopila)* plant and spikelet.

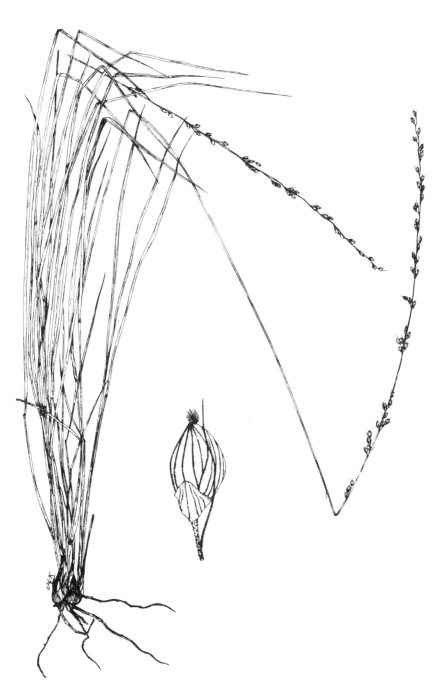

Fig. 127.   Reverchon bristlegrass *(Setaria reverchonii)* plant and spikelet.

the margins. *Blades* long and narrow, flat or more frequently inrolled when dried, usually narrower at the base than the sheath apex. *Inflorescence* a narrow, contracted, spikelike panicle 6–20 cm long, the spikelets short-stalked and erect or closely pressed against short branches. *Main axis of panicle and branches* terminated by a spikelet with a single bristle below, the other spikelets with or without bristles below. *Bristles* shorter than to considerably longer than spikelets but rarely more than 6 mm in length. *Spikelets* breaking off at their base, the bristles persistent. *Spikelets* variable in size, from 2.5–4 mm long. *First glume* about one-half as long as the second glume and the lemma of the lower floret. *Lemma of upper (seed-bearing) floret* conspicuously roughened. Plants setting seed mainly in late spring, but apparently this grass has a long flowering period.

DISTRIBUTION AND HABITAT. Reverchon bristlegrass is reported from nearly all regions except the Pineywoods, and it probably is most frequent on the rocky, well-drained limestone soils of the Edwards Plateau in the center of the state.

USE. This species is a native, warm-season perennial of fair value as a forage plant for livestock and wildlife, but it usually grows in scattered stands.

SORGHASTRUM

128. Yellow Indiangrass   *Sorghastrum nutans* (L.) Nash

Stems mostly 0.8–2.3 m tall, usually in small clumps, stiffly erect from short, stout, scaly rhizomes. *Stem nodes* bristly with stiff hairs. *Sheaths* hairless or infrequently slightly hairy, the sheath margins continued upward at the tip as stiff, membranous, pointed lateral auricles and a stiff ligule 2–5 mm long. *Blades* long, linear, flat, mostly 5–10 mm broad, tapering to a narrow base and a long, drawn-out tip. *Inflorescence* a loosely contracted, little-branched panicle 15–30 cm long. *Spikelets* in combinations of one stalkless, seed-bearing spikelet and one or two slender, hairy stalks with the spikelets entirely lacking or vestigal. *Uppermost branchlets, stalks, and glumes* hairy with stiff, silvery hairs. *Spikelets* 6–8 mm long, the glumes light brown or straw-colored. *Awn of lemma* mostly 12–17 mm long, bent and tightly twisted below the bend, loosely twisted and slightly spiraling above the bend. Plants setting seed mostly September to November.

DISTRIBUTION AND HABITAT. Yellow Indiangrass is reported from all regions of the state but is most frequent in the tall-grass prairies of central and coastal Texas.

USE. This grass is a native, warm-season perennial that provides good grazing for livestock and fair grazing for wildlife. Yellow Indiangrass, big

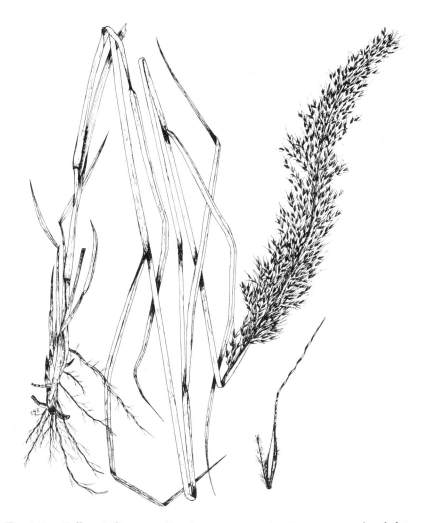

Fig. 128.   Yellow Indiangrass *(Sorghastrum nutans)* inflorescence and spikelet attached to empty spikelet stalk.

bluestem, little bluestem, and switchgrass make up the "big four" tall-grass prairie grasses in the central United States True Prairie Association. All four are important range forage species and indicators that range is in good condition. Yellow Indiangrass provides forage of high quality when it is green and of fair quality when it is mature. In some areas it is grown and managed in pure stands and responds well to fertilization and irrigation.

SORGHUM

129. Johnsongrass *Sorghum halepense* (L.) Pers.

Leafy perennial with extensive creeping rhizomes. *Stems* mostly 1–2 m tall, but much shorter in dry or otherwise unfavorable sites. *Stem nodes* hairless or finely downy. *Blades* succulent, large, linear, usually hairless, mostly 0.8–1.5 cm broad. *Panicle* typically large, open, and freely branched, mostly 15–35 cm long. *Spikelets* in pairs of one stalkless and seed-bearing spikelet and one or two stalked male (with stamens only) or neuter spikelets that are slightly smaller in size. *Stalkless spikelets* 4.5–5.5 mm long, awnless or with a delicate, bent, readily deciduous lemma awn. *Glumes of stalkless (seed-bearing) spikelet* broad, firm, nerveless, shiny except at the tip, downy at least on the margins. *Lemma awn*, when present, 1–1.5 mm long with a twisted lower segment. *Stalked spikelets* usually with stamens only, awnless, lanceolate, as long as or longer than the stalkless ones but narrower and thinner and with more strongly veined glumes. *Grain* 2–3 mm long. Plants setting seed mostly May to November, but flowering throughout the year under favorable growing conditions. Early-spring flowering plants for the most part are infected with smut.

DISTRIBUTION AND HABITAT. Johnsongrass grows throughout the state. It is cultivated as a forage grass, but it is more common as a weed of low roadsides and ditches.

USE. An introduced, warm-season perennial that provides good grazing for livestock and fair grazing for wildlife, Johnsongrass has become a serious weed pest of irrigated croplands in some areas. Although it is frequently grown for forage, this succulent perennial develops cyanide compounds under certain conditions of growth and can be the cause of prussic acid poisoning in grazing animals.

SPARTINA

Key to the species:
Panicles with two to seven loosely erect-spreading branches . . . .
. . . . Marshhay cordgrass, S. *patens*
Panicles with nine to thirty appressed branches
    Inflorescence branches fifteen to thirty, mostly 1.5–4 cm long; bunch grass without rhizomes . . . . Gulf cordgrass, S. *spartinae*
    Inflorescence branches nine to twenty, when twelve or more then at least some 5–10 cm long; stems solitary or in small clusters from thick, whitish rhizomes . . . .
. . . . Smooth cordgrass, S. *alterniflora*

Fig. 129.   Johnsongrass *(Sorghum halepense)* inflorescence and spikelet pair.

Fig. 130.   Smooth cordgrass *(Spartina alterniflora* var. *glabra)* inflorescence and spikelet.

130. Smooth cordgrass *Spartina alterniflora* Loisel. var. *glabra* (Muhl.) Fern.

Strong perennial with stems mostly 1–2 m tall, solitary or in small clumps from thick but rather soft whitish rhizomes. *Leaves* essentially hairless, the ligule a minute fringe of hairs. *Sheaths* rounded, the lower sheaths often broad and inflated. *Blades* thick, flat at least near their base, mostly 5–12 mm broad. *Panicles* 15–35 cm long, with nine to twenty erect branches, these loosely arranged on a stout central axis. *Spikelets* 8–14 mm long. *Glumes* unequal, hairless, awnless or tipped abruptly with a short awn, the nerves smooth or occasionally with a few prickle-hairs. *First glume* often more than one-half as long as the second. *Lemmas* hairless, shorter than the paleas. *Anthers* 4–6 mm long. Plants setting seed mostly July to November.

DISTRIBUTION AND HABITAT. Smooth cordgrass grows along the coast, usually in standing water or in saturated muddy soils on tide flats and bayou margins.

USE. This grass is of little significance as a forage plant, but it helps provide habitat for coastal birds and in general contributes to the coastal marsh-estuary habitat.

One readily recognizable characteristic of smooth cordgrass is the somewhat disagreeable odor of the freshly crushed herbage which persists for some time on dried specimens.

131. Marshhay cordgrass *Spartina patens* (Ait.) Muhl.

Stems 0.5–1.5 m tall, single or in small clusters from creeping rhizomes or in large clumps from a base not forming rhizomes. *Blades* narrow, tightly inrolled when dried, 1–2 mm broad on the more slender, rhizome-forming plants, 2–4 mm broad on the more coarse, vigorous bunch types. *Inflorescences* of the slender, rhizome-forming plants with two or three, and infrequently up to five, branches, the coarser bunched plants with usually four to seven branches. *Inflorescence branches* slender, 3–8 cm long. *Spikelets* mostly 7–12 mm long. *Glumes* awnless, the first glume usually less than half the length of the spikelet, the second glume as long as the spikelet. *Lemmas and paleas* blunt, the paleas slightly longer than the lemmas. Plants setting seed mostly May to September, but occasionally flowering at other times.

DISTRIBUTION AND HABITAT. Marshhay cordgrass is frequent along the coast, with the slender, rhizome-forming type widespread and common on beaches, sandy flats, and low dunes and the coarse bunch type occurring along muddy bayous and marshlands of the northeastern Texas coast, usually in the tidewater zone.

USE. Marshhay cordgrass is a native, warm-season perennial providing good grazing for livestock but poor grazing for wildlife. It decreases with heavy grazing.

Fig. 131.   Marshhay cordgrass *(Spartina patens)* inflorescence.

216 : Common Texas Grasses

132. Gulf cordgrass *Spartina spartinae* (Trin.) Merr.

Stout perennial bunch grass with firm or tough stems in dense clumps from a base that does not form rhizomes. *Leaves and stems* hairless or essentially so. *Sheaths* broad, rounded on the back. *Blades* thick, stiff, short, narrower than the sheaths, inrolled when dried, with a sharp-pointed tip. *Inflorescences* stout, spikelike, mostly 15–25 cm long and with branches 1.5–4 cm long, the branches closely placed and tightly pressed along the main axis. *Spikelets* 6–8 mm long. *Glumes* rough or short-fringed on the keel, the first glume narrow, usually about half or less as long as the second. *Second glume* blunt or slightly notched, often short-awned. *Lemmas* blunt, rough on the keel, awnless or abruptly short-awned, slightly shorter than the paleas. Plants setting seed summer and fall.

DISTRIBUTION AND HABITAT. Gulf cordgrass is frequent on Gulf coastal flats, on old dunes, and along brackish marshlands; it is occasional in salt flats and marshes at interior locations in the southern half of the state. Gulf cordgrass forms extensive meadows along the coastal salt flats and other lowland areas. It often grows in soils that occasionally are submerged.

USE. This grass is a native, warm-season perennial providing fair grazing for livestock and poor grazing for wildlife.

SPOROBOLUS

Key to the species:
Plants without long, scaly, creeping rhizomes; plants of the seashore or not
  Glumes unequal, the second about as long as the spikelet
    Spikelets mostly 4–6 mm long .... *S. asper*
    Spikelets mostly 1.5–2.8 mm long
      Panicles 15–35 cm long, well exserted from or partially enclosed in the sheath, the lower branches not in whorls
        Base of plant thick, firm or hard; panicles 15–25 cm broad, usually well exserted from the sheath; stalks and branchlets of the panicle spreading ....
        .... Alkali sacaton, *S. airoides*
        Base of plant not thick, not firm or hard; panicles 2–12 cm broad, often partially or nearly totally enclosed in the sheath; branchlets of the panicle appressed ....
        .... Sand dropseed, *S. cryptandrus*
      Panicles mostly 3–15 cm long, well exserted from the sheath, the lower branches in whorls ....
      .... Whorled dropseed, *S. pyramidatus*
  Glumes about equal, one-third to one-half as long as the spikelet ......
  .... Rattail smutgrass, *S. indicus*

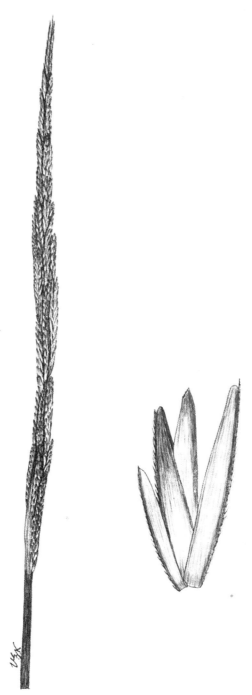

Fig. 132.   Gulf cordgrass *(Spartina spartinae)* inflorescence and spikelet.

Plants with long, scaly, creeping rhizomes; plants of the seashore · · · · ·
· Seashore dropseed, S. *virginicus*

Fig. 133. Alkali sacaton *(Sporobolus airoides)* plant and spikelet with glumes separated from floret.

133. Alkali sacaton *Sporobolus airoides* (Torr.) Torr.

Coarse perennial bunch grass with numerous erect, firm, tough stems arising from a hard base. *Stems* hairless, shining, 50–150 cm tall and 1–3 mm in diameter at the base. *Sheaths* rounded, often with a few white hairs 2–4 mm long on the margins on either side of the collar. *Blades* flat or becoming inrolled, 15–45 cm long, 2–6 mm wide. *Panicles* 20–45 cm long and 15–25 cm broad, usually open and diffuse, somewhat pyramidal in shape. *Spikelets* purplish or greenish, 1.3–2.5 mm long, mostly on spreading stalks 0.5–2 mm long, the branchlets naked at their base. *Glumes* unequal, the first usually 0.4–1.8 mm long and acute, and the second usually 1–2.5 mm long. *Lemma and palea* about as long as the second glume. *Anthers* yellowish, mostly 1.5–1.7 mm long. *Grain* about 1 mm long, with reddish or blackish streaks. Plants setting seed June to November.

DISTRIBUTION AND HABITAT. Alkali sacaton grows in the north-central, central, and western portions of the state on dry sandy or gravelly slopes and along saline or alkaline flats.

USE. Although alkali sacaton is only of fair value for livestock grazing and of low value for wildlife grazing, it is a desirable grass to establish as cover in "salted out" areas.

134. *Sporobolus asper* (Michx.) Kunth

Perennial with spikelets in narrow terminal panicles and often with self-fertilized (cleistogamous) spikelets in short panicles in the upper leaf sheaths. *Stems* slender, erect, solitary or in small clumps, mostly 60–120 cm tall. *Sheaths* hairless or the lower ones soft-haired near the collar. *Blades* elongate, flat or folded, hairless or the lower ones hairy, mostly 1–4 mm wide. *Inflorescence* a contracted, spikelike panicle 5–30 cm long and 4–12 mm wide, often partially enclosed within a somewhat inflated sheath. *Spikelets* 4–6 mm long, mostly densely crowded on the panicle branches, these tightly pressed along the main axis. *Glumes* silvery, pale green or purplish, somewhat keeled, usually with a bright green mid-nerve, the first glume slightly more than one-half as long to nearly as long as the second glume. *Lemmas* blunt at the tip, usually longer than the second glume, hairless. *Grains* mostly 1.6–2 mm long, about 1 mm wide, reddish brown, plump. *Seed* separating from the ovary wall and becoming sticky when moistened. Plants setting seed mostly September to November.

Key to the varieties:
Stems mostly 1–2 mm thick near the base; terminal sheath mostly
    0.8–2 mm broad when folded; primary panicle branches eight to
    eighteen . . . . Meadow dropseed, *S. asper* var. *drummondii*
Stems 2–5 mm thick near the base; terminal sheath 1.5–6 mm broad when
    folded; primary panicle branches twelve to thirty-five . . . .
    . . . . Tall dropseed, *S. asper* var. *asper*

134a. Tall dropseed *Sporobolus asper* (Michx.) Kunth var. *asper*

DISTRIBUTION AND HABITAT. This variety has the same general distribution and time of flowering as meadow dropseed but tends to be more common on open, rocky prairie sites.

Fig. 134a. Tall dropseed *(Sporobolus asper* var. *asper)* plant and spikelet.

USE. Tall dropseed is a native, warm-season perennial that provides fair grazing for livestock and wildlife.

134b. Meadow dropseed *Sporobolus asper* (Michx.) Kunth var. *drummondii* (Trin.) Vasey

Similar to tall dropseed, but the stems more slender and the upper sheaths and panicles smaller.

DISTRIBUTION AND HABITAT. Occurring throughout the state except in the extreme west and northwest, and often found in open woodlands, meadow dropseed grows best on heavy soils that occasionally receive extra moisture.

USE. This native, warm-season perennial provides fair grazing for livestock and poor grazing for wildlife.

Meadow dropseed has long gone under the scientific name of *Sporobolus asper* var. *hookeri* (Trin.) Vasey, a name that now is considered a synonym.

135. Sand dropseed *Sporobolus cryptandrus* (Torr.) A. Gray

Tufted perennial with slender, erect stems mostly 35–120 cm tall but occasionally shorter. *Sheaths* rounded, usually with tufts of long, white hairs on either side of the collar and often fringed with hairs on the upper margins. *Blades* mostly 8–25 cm long and 2–5 mm wide, usually flat but often folded or inrolled when dried, hairless, not stiffly spreading from the stem. *Panicles* 15–30 cm long and 2–12 cm wide, usually narrow and partially enclosed by the elongated upper sheath. *Panicle main axis* slender but often stiffly erect, the primary branches borne singly at the nodes, bunched or spreading, with spikelets nearly to the base or the branches naked on the lower 5–10 mm. *Secondary branches and branchlets* closely pressed against the primary branches. *Spikelets* short-stalked, light brown, lead-colored, or purple-tinged, 1.5–2.5 mm long. *Glumes* thin, membranous, acute, the first glume about half as long as the second and the second equaling or slightly shorter than the lemma. *Grains* reddish orange, oblong, flattened laterally, about 1 mm long. Plants setting seed mostly May to November.

DISTRIBUTION AND HABITAT. Sand dropseed grows throughout the state except in the Pineywoods. It is frequent on sandy soils and is one of the most common roadside perennial grasses.

USE. A native, warm-season perennial that provides fair grazing for livestock and poor grazing for wildlife, this species is an invader on sandy soil in overgrazed or "blown-out" areas.

136. Rattail smutgrass *Sporobolus indicus* (L.) R. Br. (*Sporobolus poiretii* [R. & S.] Hitchc.)

Tufted perennial with tough, fibrous roots and narrow, hairless stems

Fig. 135. Sand dropseed *(Sporobolus cryptandrus)* plant and spikelet with glumes separated from floret.

and leaves. *Stems* stiffly erect, mostly 30–100 cm tall, unbranched above the base. *Leaves* mostly in a basal tuft. *Blades* flat, folded or inrolled, mostly 10–30 cm long and 1–5 mm broad at their base, tapering to a long, wavy, threadlike tip. *Inflorescence* a long, narrow, tightly contracted panicle with all the branches short and erect or a few of the lower branches erect or spreading. *Panicle* 10–35 cm long and 0.6–1 cm broad. *Panicle branches* densely flowered to their base, mostly 1–2 cm long but

Fig. 136.   Rattail smutgrass *(Sporobolus indicus)* inflorescence and spikelet.

occasionally as much as 3–5 cm long. *Spikelets* awnless, 1.4–2 mm long. *Glumes* thin, nearly equal, about one-half as long as the lemma. *Lemmas and paleas* of the same texture as the glumes. *Grains* reddish brown, obovate, flattened laterally, somewhat chopped off at the tip. Plants setting seed mostly March to December.

DISTRIBUTION AND HABITAT. Rattail smutgrass is found in the eastern third of the state, mostly on moist clay soils but also in sand, and often in trampled or otherwise disturbed sites.

USE. This grass is a coarse, warm-season perennial that provides poor grazing for both livestock and wildlife.

137. Whorled dropseed   *Sporobolus pyramidatus* (Lam.) Hitchc.

Tufted perennial. *Stems* numerous, slender, mostly 10–50 cm tall, branching only at the base. *Sheaths* shorter than the stem internodes, hairless except for long white hairs on either side of the collar. *Blades* mostly basal, 3–12 cm (occasionally up to 20 cm) long and usually 2–4 mm wide, fringed with hairs on the lower margins and often sparsely hairy on the upper surface. *Inflorescence* a panicle 3–15 cm long, contracted at first but becoming pyramidal, with branches successively shorter from the base upward. *Lower panicle branches* in whorls, naked on the lower one-third to one-half. *Spikelets* one-flowered, awnless, 1.5–2 mm long. *Glumes* thin, acute, the first usually 0.3–0.8 mm long and the second mostly 1.2–2 mm long. *Lemmas* acute, 1.2–2 mm long. *Palea* translucent, about as long as the lemma, splitting as the grain matures. *Grains* 0.6–0.9 mm long, broadly oblong, pale orange and translucent, finely streaked. Plants setting seed mostly March to November.

DISTRIBUTION AND HABITAT. Whorled dropseed grows throughout the state except in the East Texas Pineywoods. It occurs in open, usually disturbed sites on a wide variety of soil types and frequently on coastal sands and on sandy or saline clay or alkaline inland soils.

USE. This species is a somewhat weedy native, warm-season, short-lived perennial with little or no significance as a forage grass.

138. Seashore dropseed   *Sporobolus virginicus* (L.) Kunth

Perennial with stems arising singly or in small clusters from widely spreading, usually yellowish rhizomes. *Stems* with several to many nodes, smooth and shining, 10–50 cm tall. *Sheaths* mostly overlapping, streaked, hairless except for a few long hairs on either side of the collar. *Ligule* a minute, fringed membrane, 0.2–0.5 mm long. *Blades* firm, usually inrolled at least when dried, mostly 3–12 cm long and 1.5–4 mm wide, often in a conspicuous double row. *Inflorescence* a contracted, spikelike, densely flowered panicle mostly 2–8 cm long and 6–8 mm wide. *Spikelets* one-flowered, awnless, straw-colored, grayish, or purple-tinged, hairless, shining, 1.8–3.2 mm long. *First glume* two-thirds the length of or equal to

Fig. 137. Whorled dropseed *(Sporobolus pyramidatus)* inflorescence and spikelet.

the second glume. *Second glume* 1.8–3.2 mm long, equaling or slightly longer than the lemma. Plants setting seed May to October, occasionally as late as December.

DISTRIBUTION AND HABITAT. Seashore dropseed occurs along the coast on sandy beaches and at the base of sand dunes.

USE. This coarse, native, warm-season perennial is widely distributed and frequent along the Gulf, but it probably is little grazed by cattle or wildlife. The main value of seashore dropseed is in its function as a soil stabilizer along the sandy shores.

226 : Common Texas Grasses

Fig. 138.   Seashore dropseed *(Sporobolus virginicus)* plant and spikelet.

Fig. 139. St. Augustinegrass *(Stenotaphrum secundatum)* plant and spikelet.

STENOTAPHRUM

139. St. Augustinegrass *Stenotaphrum secundatum* (Walt.) Kuntze

Low, mat-forming, stolon-forming perennial. *Stems* spreading and upward-curving, creeping, much-branched, with erect flowering branches 10–30 cm tall. *Leaves* bright green, succulent, hairless or the sheaths sparsely fringed on the upper margins. *Blades* thick, flat, mostly 3–15 mm long and 4–10 mm broad but longer on sterile shoots, blunt and rounded at the tip. *Inflorescence* spikelike, 5–10 cm long, with short, stout, closely placed and bunched branches, each bearing one to three stalkless or short-stalked spikelets. *Spikelets* partially embedded in one

228 : Common Texas Grasses

side of a broad, thick, flattened inflorescence axis, breaking apart at the axis nodes, the spikelets falling attached to sections of the axis. Spikelets 4–5 mm long, two-flowered, the lower floret male (with stamens only) or neuter, the upper floret seed-bearing. *First glume* short but well developed, irregularly rounded. *Second glume and lemma of lower floret* about equal, hairless, awnless, faintly nerved, pointed at the tip. *Lemma of upper (seed bearing) floret* ovate, awnless, pointed, with thin, flat margins. Plants flowering throughout the summer and early autumn, but seldom perfecting good seed.

DISTRIBUTION AND HABITAT. St. Augustinegrass grows in the eastern, central, and southern portions of the state, frequently as a grass of lawns and parks and also spontaneously in moist soil along stream courses and lakeshores and in swales. Reproduction in St. Augustinegrass is almost entirely by sprigging or cloning.

USE. St. Augustinegrass and Bermudagrass are the two most common lawn grasses in Texas. St. Augustinegrass basically is less aggressive than Bermudagrass, but with watering and fertilization it will replace Bermudagrass, especially in partial shade. Although it is rather coarse in texture, St. Augustinegrass has the additional advantage of forming stolons and not rhizomes. It also tends to be less susceptible to infestation by chiggers and redbugs.

STIPA

Key to the species:
Glumes 20–33 mm long; lemma awns 10–20 cm long . . . .
. . . . Needle-and-thread, *S. comata*
Glumes 14–18 mm long; lemma awns 4.5–10 cm long . . . .
. . . . Texas wintergrass, *S. leucotricha*

140. Needle-and-thread *Stipa comata* Trin. & Rupr.
Tufted perennial with stems mostly 30–70 cm (sometimes up to 110 cm) tall, in dense clumps. *Leaves and stems* without hairs. *Blades* flat, long and threadlike, infolded or inrolled, mostly 15–30 cm (occasionally as much as 40 cm) long and 1–2 mm broad. *Inflorescence* a loose panicle of large, one-flowered, long-awned spikelets. *Glumes* thin, with five to seven nerves, about equal, 20–33 mm long, with long, narrow, pointed tips. *Lemma* firm, tightly enclosing the palea, 10–15 mm long, the base of the body and the callus densely bearded with stiff hairs, the body sparsely long-haired to nearly hairless, the tip without hairs. *Lemma awns* 10–20 cm long, faintly twice-bent, twisted and short-haired on the lower half, hairless or nearly so on the upper segment, persistent or deciduous. Plants setting seed mostly May to July.

Fig. 140.   Needle-and-thread *(Stipa comata)* plant, glumes, and floret.

DISTRIBUTION AND HABITAT. Needle-and-thread is rather frequent on the open rolling grasslands and rocky outcrops on the High Plains of northwestern Texas, and it is occasional in the mountains of Trans-Pecos Texas.

USE. This grass is a native perennial of fair value as a forage plant for livestock and of poor value for wildlife.

141. Texas wintergrass   *Stipa leucotricha* Trin. & Rupr.
Tufted perennial with erect or spreading stems 30–70 cm (or up to 90

Fig. 141. Texas wintergrass (*Stipa leucotricha*) inflorescence and spikelet.

cm) tall. *Stem nodes* with short, erect hairs, becoming hairless with age. *Sheaths* variously hairy to nearly hairless, the collar usually with long hairs on the sides. *Blades* mostly 10–30 cm long and 1–5 mm broad, flat or loosely infolded, usually with short, stiff hairs on one or both surfaces. *Inflorescence* a loose panicle mostly 6–25 cm long with long, slender lower branches. *Glumes* thin, hairless, about equal or the first longer,

14–18 mm long, with five to seven nerves and long, narrow tips. *First glume* three-nerved. *Second glume* with three to five nerves. *Base of lemma* sharp-pointed, densely hairy. *Lemma* 9–12 mm long, light brown, rough on the body above the base, with a rounded, whitish neck 0.6–1 mm long, this neck fringed on top with a ring of stiff hairs but otherwise hairless. *Awn of lemma* stout, loosely bent once or twice, 4.5–10 cm long. Plants setting seed mostly March to May or June, but occasionally later in cool sites.

DISTRIBUTION AND HABITAT. Texas wintergrass grows throughout the state, but it is most frequent in open grassland sites of central and southern Texas, growing on both sandy and clayey soils.

USE. A native, cool-season perennial, Texas wintergrass provides fair grazing for both livestock and wildlife. It thrives under conditions of moderate disturbance and is frequently abundant on roadsides and in heavily grazed pastures. It is not highly tolerant of shade. Although it is of considerable value for early spring green forage, the growing period for this grass is relatively short.

TRACHYPOGON

142. Crinkleawn *Trachypogon secundus* (Presl) Scribn.

Tufted perennial with stems 60–120 cm tall. *Stem nodes* densely bearded, becoming hairless in age. *Sheaths* rounded on the back or slightly keeled, those of the lower and middle leaves continued at the apex into a brownish membranous ligule 1–10 mm long, those of the upper leaves with a short, fringed ligule. *Blades* linear, mostly 1–6 mm broad, those of the lower leaves 20–30 cm long. *Inflorescence* a spikelike raceme 10–20 cm long. *Spikelets* in pairs on a persistent axis, one nearly stalkless and awnless and one with a slightly longer stalk and awn, breaking up at the base of the longer-stalked, perfect (seed-bearing) spikelet. *Short-stalked spikelet* male (with stamens only), 6–8 mm long, with a large, firm outer glume that is sparsely bristled to downy and rounded on the back. *Longer-stalked (seed-bearing) spikelet* about the same length and appearance as the short-stalked one, but the lemma with a stout awn 4–6 cm long. *Lemma awn* loosely twisted and contorted, densely feathery below with hairs mostly 2–5 mm long. Plants setting seed mostly September to November.

DISTRIBUTION AND HABITAT. Crinkleawn occurs along the Gulf Coast and in the southern and western parts of the state, mostly in loose, sandy soils or on rocky slopes.

USE. This grass is a native, warm-season perennial that provides good grazing for livestock and fair grazing for wildlife.

Fig. 142.   Crinkleawn *(Trachypogon secundus)* plant and spikelet.

TRIDENS

Key to the species:
Panicles contracted, densely flowered, elongated and spikelike
    Nerves of the lemmas without hairs .... White tridens, *T. albescens*
    Nerves of the lemmas hairy, at least below the middle ... *T. muticus*
Panicles open, loosely flowered, not spikelike .... Purpletop, *T. flavus*

143. White tridens   *Tridens albescens* (Vasey) Woot. & Standl.

    Tufted perennial with stems mostly 30–90 cm tall from a hard, often knotty and rhizomatous base. *Stems* hairless or with the lowermost nodes sparsely bearded. *Sheaths* rounded on the back or the lower ones somewhat compressed laterally, without hairs. *Blades* firm, hairless, short or somewhat elongate, 1–4 mm broad, often loosely infolded when dried, with long, pointed, inrolled tips. *Inflorescence* a densely flowered, contracted panicle, 8–25 cm long and 0.6–1.5 cm thick, with short, closely appressed branches, the lowermost 2–6 cm long. *Spikelets* short-stalked, 4–10 mm long, with four to eleven flowers, mostly straw-colored, but the lemma tips usually purple and the spikelets thus appearing banded. *Glumes* thin, broad, single-nerved, pointed, nearly equal and about as long as the lower lemmas. *Lemmas* thin and papery, hairless, 3–4 mm long, often purple-tinged at the broad, slightly notched tip. Plants setting seed March to November.

    DISTRIBUTION AND HABITAT. White tridens is found throughout the state except in the Pineywoods of eastern Texas. It usually grows in clayey soils along ditches, in swales, and in other areas that periodically receive an abundance of drainage water.

    USE. White tridens is a native, warm-season perennial that provides fair grazing for both livestock and wildlife.

144. Purpletop   *Tridens flavus* (L.) Hitchc.

    Tall, slender, perennial bunch grass with a firm, often knotty base. *Stems* mostly 0.6–1.8 m tall, hairless. *Sheaths* hairy on the collar, otherwise smooth, the lower sheaths laterally compressed and keeled. *Blades* elongate, usually with a few hairs in the vicinity of the ligule, mostly 3–10 mm broad, tapering to a long point, inrolled at the tip. *Inflorescence* an open, often drooping panicle 15–35 cm or more long and with erect-spreading or widely spreading lower branches 10–25 cm long. *Branches* bare of spikelets for the basal one-third to one-half of their length. *Spikelets* 5–9 mm long, with four to eight flowers, short-stalked and loosely clustered on the branchlets, often minutely awned. *Lemmas* thin but firm, 3–5 mm long, three-nerved, the lateral nerves fringed with hairs to well above the middle. *Tip of lemma* usually notched and with a

Fig. 143.   White tridens *(Tridens albescens)* plant, spikelet, and floret.

Fig. 144. Purpletop *(Tridens flavus)* plant, inflorescence, and spikelet.

minute awn, the lateral nerves of at least some lemmas extended as minute awns. Plants setting seed late August to November.

DISTRIBUTION AND HABITAT. Purpletop grows almost throughout the state but is absent from the South Texas Plains. It is found mostly in partial shade of open woods or along roadways through woods.

USE. Purpletop is a native, warm-season perennial that provides fair grazing for both livestock and wildlife.

145. *Tridens muticus* (Torr.) Nash
Tufted perennial with stiffly erect stems mostly 20–80 cm tall. *Stem*

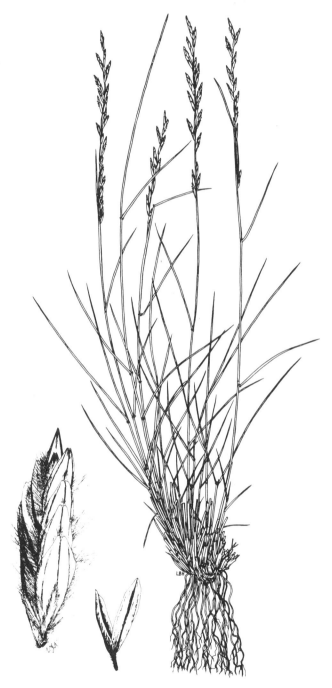

Fig. 145b.   Slim tridens *(Tridens muticus* var. *muticus)* plant and spikelet with glumes separated from florets.

nodes often bearded with long, soft hairs. *Sheaths* rounded on the back, the upper one hairless, the lower ones often soft-haired. *Blades* 6–25 cm long and 1–4 mm broad, hairless or with soft, straight hairs, usually loosely infolded when dried, gradually tapering to a long tip. *Inflorescence* a narrow, contracted, elongated panicle, mostly 7–20 cm long and 3–8 mm thick, with the spikelets short-stalked, tightly appressed and closely placed but usually not crowded or congested. *Spikelets* 8–13 mm long, with five to eleven flowers, awnless, usually purple-tinged. *Glumes* without hairs, with one to seven nerves, pointed, about equal in length or the first shorter than the second, the second nearly as long as the lower lemma. *Lemmas* 3.5–5.5 mm long, fringed on the midnerve to about the middle and on the two lateral nerves to well above the middle, obtuse or slightly notched at the tip. *Grain* oblong, finely roughened, mostly 2–2.3 mm long. Plants setting seed mostly July to November, but occasionally earlier.

Key to the varieties:
Second glume with three to seven nerves, typically 6–8 mm long . . . . .
. . . . Rough tridens, *T. muticus* var. *elongatus*
Second glume single-nerved, typically but not always 5 mm or less long . . .
. . . . Slim tridens, *T. muticus* var. *muticus*

145a. Rough tridens *Tridens muticus* (Torr.) Nash var. *elongatus* (Buckl.) Shinners

DISTRIBUTION AND HABITAT. Rough tridens is found in the central and north-central portions of the state on open rangelands, usually in sandy soil.

USE. Rough tridens is a native, warm-season perennial that occurs in scattered stands and provides fair forage for livestock and wildlife.

145b. Slim tridens *Tridens muticus* (Torr.) Nash var. *muticus*

DISTRIBUTION AND HABITAT. Slim tridens is widespread throughout the state except in the Pineywoods, mostly in rocky or sandy open soil.

USE. This grass is a native, warm-season perennial that provides fair grazing for both livestock and wildlife.

TRIPSACUM

146. Eastern gamagrass *Tripsacum dactyloides* (L.) L.

Tall bunch grass with stems 1.5–3 m or more tall in large clumps from thick, knotty rhizomes. *Stems and leaves* hairless. *Sheaths* rounded, smooth and shiny. *Ligule* a short, fringed or irregular-edged membrane. *Blades* thin, flat, mostly 10–25 mm broad and 30–75 cm or more long. *Inflorescence* a spike 12–25 cm long or of two or three erect, spikelike

Fig. 146.   Eastern gamagrass *(Tripsacum dactyloides)* inflorescence with female (pistillate) spikelets below the male (staminate) ones.

branches. *Spike or spikelike branches* with a stiff axis bearing male spikelets (with stamens only) above and female (seed-bearing) spikelets below. *Male spikelets* awnless, two-flowered, mostly 6–10 mm long, in pairs on one side of a persistent central axis. *Glumes of male spikelets* membranous, flat, several-nerved. *Female spikelets* short-stalked, usually solitary, with hard and bony awnless glumes mostly 6–8 mm long, the glumes fused with the central axis and tightly enclosing the other spikelet parts. *Lemmas* of female spikelets thin and translucent, often reduced. *Stalks and stalked spikelets* usually absent, a rudiment occasionally present. *Male portion of inflorescence* deciduous as a whole, the female portion breaking up at the nodes into hard, shiny, beadlike units. Plants setting seed April to November.

DISTRIBUTION AND HABITAT. Eastern gamagrass occurs throughout the state, but it is most frequent in the eastern portion, mostly in low, moist, little-disturbed grassland sites.

USE. A native, warm-season perennial providing good forage for livestock and wildlife, eastern gamagrass responds well to fertilization and can be grown in pure stands as a pasture grass.

TRITICUM

147. Wheat *Triticum aestivum* L.

Annual with stiffly erect, hollow stems mostly 60–100 cm tall. *Sheaths* thin, rounded, usually with slender auricles on either side of the collar. *Ligule* a membrane 1–3 cm long. *Blades* elongate, 0.7–2 cm long (excluding the awns when present), the spikelets double-ranked and closely overlapped on a stout, persistent axis. *Spikelets* mostly 10–15 mm long (excluding the awns when these are present), with two to five flowers, hairless or hairy, awned or awnless, breaking up above the glumes and between the florets, laterally flattened and oriented with their flat side toward the axis. *Glumes* usually strongly keeled toward one side, the keel often with a stout awn 6 cm or more long. *Lemmas* keeled or rounded on the back, awnless with a stout, rough awn to 15 cm long. *Grain* ovate or oblong, usually hairy at the tip. Plants setting seed mostly March to May.

DISTRIBUTION AND HABITAT. Wheat is grown in Texas as a cool-season crop plant, and it occurs as a weed of roadsides and waste places throughout the state. It is frequent as a wayside grass in agricultural areas, but it has never actually become established outside of cultivation.

USE. Wheat as a casual annual, introduced, cool-season roadside weed probably does not contribute significantly as a forage plant. In the northern part of Texas, however, seeded wheat fields are often first used as pasture and then allowed to mature for the grain. When it is cut, green wheat is an excellent forage plant for livestock. Wheat straw, cut after the grain has matured, has little nutritional value but is often fed with supplement.

UNIOLA

148. Seaoats *Uniola paniculata* L.

Perennial with tall, stout stems developed singly or in small clumps

Fig. 147. Wheat *(Triticum aestivum)* inflorescence.

from long, thick rhizomes. *Stems* hairless, mostly 1–2.2 m tall, branching only at the base. *Leaves* firm and tough in texture, a few of the basal ones reduced and scalelike. *Sheaths* rounded or the lowermost slightly keeled, hairless. *Blades* linear, flat or folded at the base, inrolled at the slender, elongated tips, 80 cm or more long and 5–10 mm broad at the base. *Inflorescence* a contracted panicle, typically 20–50 cm long and 5–10 cm

Fig. 148. Seaoats *(Uniola paniculata)* inflorescence.

broad, with relatively short, slender branches, the lower ones drooping at maturity under the weight of the large spikelets. *Spikelets* with twelve to twenty florets, broad, laterally compressed and sharply keeled, for the most part smooth and shiny, the lower few florets sterile, 1.5–3.5 cm long. *Spikelets* not readily breaking apart, but at length breaking off below the glumes and falling as a whole. *Glumes* firm, nearly equal, with three to five indistinct nerves, pointed at the tips. *Lemmas* broad, keeled, pointed, awnless, with three to nine nerves, finely toothed on the keels and often minutely fringed with hairs on the margins. *Paleas* about as long as the lemmas, the two keels winged. *Grains* elongate, 3–5 mm long.

Fig. 149. Common sixweeksgrass *(Vulpia octoflora)* plant and spikelet.

Plants setting seed June to December, but mostly flowering in late summer and early autumn.

DISTRIBUTION AND HABITAT. Seaoats is found along the coast on dunes and sandy flats along the ocean.

USE. Seaoats is a native, warm-season perennial that is a valuable soil binder and dune stabilizer along the Gulf Coast. It has essentially no forage value for livestock.

VULPIA

149. Common sixweeksgrass *Vulpia octoflora* (Walt.) Rydb.
    Short-lived annual with slender, weak, solitary or loosely tufted

Fig. 150. Southern wildrice *(Zizaniopsis miliacea)* inflorescence, male spikelet (below), female spikelet (middle), and caryopsis (above).

stems mostly 10–50 cm tall. *Blades* up to 10 cm long, 0.5–1 mm broad, hairless or hairy. *Inflorescence* usually a narrow, more-or-less contracted panicle or raceme 1–20 cm long, usually with short, closely appressed branches. *Spikelets* hairless or downy, 4–10 mm long excluding the awns, with five to seventeen florets, the uppermost reduced. *Lemma of lower- most floret* 2.7–6.5 mm long, with an awn 0.3–6 mm long. *Grain* narrow and elongate, brown at maturity, 1.7–3.3 mm long. Plants setting seed March to May.

DISTRIBUTION AND HABITAT. Common sixweeksgrass grows throughout the state except in the South Texas Plains. It often grows with little barley on loose, disturbed soils as a common roadside weed.

USE. This species is a short-lived, native, cool-season annual of no significance as a forage grass.

ZIZANIOPSIS

150. Southern wildrice *Zizaniopsis miliacea* (Michx.) Doell and Asch.

Coarse perennial, with thick stems from rhizomes, mostly 2–3 m tall. *Ligule* membranous, with numerous fine nerves, mostly 6–20 mm long. *Blades* without hairs, mostly 8–22 mm broad and 1 m or more long, with coarsely saw-toothed margins. *Inflorescence* a large, open panicle 30–60 cm long, with numerous freely rebranched, erect and spreading branches bearing erect, one-flowered male and female (seed-bearing) spikelets on the same branch or branchlet, the male spikelets below the female ones. *Spikelets* 6–8 mm long, with a thin, seven-nerved lemma, a thin, three-nerved palea, and without glumes. Spikelets falling entire at maturity. *Male spikelets* awnless, with six stamens. *Lemma of female spikelet* with a short, abrupt tip or short awn. *Grain* globose, about 3 mm long. Plants setting seed mostly April to July, occasionally later.

DISTRIBUTION AND HABITAT. Southern wildrice is rather common in the eastern, central, and southern portions of the state, growing in shallow fresh or brackish water along streams, lakes, and marshes.

USE. A conspicuous native, cool-season perennial often forming large colonies in shallow water and sometimes clogging waterways and lakeshores, southern wildrice is of little value as a forage plant but does provide food (grain) and cover for many forms of wildlife.

Key to the Genera of the Grasses

Spikelets unisexual, the male and female spikelets conspicuously different
  Plants with male and female spikelets in separate spikelets but on the same plant; stems tall and coarse
    Male and female spikelets in separate inflorescences . . . .
    . . . . (ZEA)
    Male and female spikelets in the same inflorescence
      Male spikelets above the female spikelets in a spike or on two or three spikelike branches . . . . TRIPSACUM
      Male spikelets below the female spikelets in a freely branched and rebranched panicle . . . . ZIZANIOPSIS
  Plants with the male spikelets on different plants; low, stoloniferous, mat-forming perennials
    Male and female spikelets awnless, the female spikelets in burlike clusters hidden in leafy portions of the plant, the male spikelets stalkless on one to four short, spikelike branches of a well-elevated inflorescence . . . . BUCHLOË
    Male spikelets awnless, the female spikelets long-awned (each lemma three-awned); both male and female spikelets in contracted, usually spikelike racemes . . . . SCLEROPOGON
Spikelets, at least some, with both stamens and pistils, or if unisexual, then the male and female spikelets not conspicuously different
  Inflorescence a spike or spikelike raceme or with two to several simple (unbranched) primary branches
    Inflorescence a spike or spikelike raceme . . . . Group I
    Inflorescence with two to several simple (unbranched) primary branches . . . . Group II
  Inflorescence with at least some spikelets on secondary as well as primary branches
    Spikelets with one bisexual floret or one male or one female floret . . .
    . . . . Group III
    Spikelets with two or more bisexual florets or two or more male or female florets . . . . Group IV

Group I (spike or spikelike raceme)

Spikelets in small, headlike spikes, these hidden in the leafy part of the tufted plant; forming stolons .... BUCHLOË
Spikelets in elongated spikes, not hidden in leafy portion of the plant
  Inflorescence a bilateral spike or raceme, the spikelets not all oriented on one side of the axis
    Spikelets with two to several well-developed bisexual florets
      Spikelets one per node of the spikelet axis
        First glume absent on all but the terminal spikelet; spikelets oriented edgewise to the spikelet axis .... LOLIUM
        First glume present on all spikelets; spikelets not oriented edgewise to the spikelet axis
          Spikelets stalked .... DISTICHLIS
          Spikelets stalkless
            Glumes firm but not thick; perennial forming rhizomes ...
            .... AGROPYRON
            Glumes thick and hard; plants annual .... TRITICUM
      Spikelets two or three per node of the spikelet axis
        Spikelets awnless, breaking off in a cluster from a persistent spikelet axis .... HILARIA
        Spikelets awned, breaking off above the glumes ..... ELYMUS
    Spikelets with one well-developed bisexual floret, with or without reduced florets
    Spikelets awnless
      Spikelets in an involucre of bristles and/or flattened spines .....
      .... CENCHRUS
      Spikelets not in an involucre of bristles or spines ....
      .... ELYONURUS
    Spikelets awned, not in involucres
      Spikelets in threes at each node of the spike axis ... HORDEUM
      Spikelets in pairs at each node, with one or both short-stalked
        Spikelet awns more than 3 cm long .... TRACHYPOGON
        Spikelet awns less than 3 cm long .... SCHIZACHYRIUM
  Inflorescence a unilateral spike or spikelike raceme; the spikelets oriented on one side of the spike axis; spikelets with a single bisexual floret
    Awns developed on at least some spikelets
      Awns 3–8 cm long
        Awned spikelets stalkless, the glumes and awns dark brown at maturity .... HETEROPOGON
        Awned spikelets stalked, the glumes and awns light-colored....
        .... TRACHYPOGON
      Awns less than 3 cm long .... BOUTELOUA

Awns absent on all spikelets

Spikelets 2.6 mm or less long, broadly rounded at the tip . . . . . .
. . . . PASPALUM

Spikelets, at least the stalkless ones, 3–6 mm long, pointed at the tip

First glume smooth, less than half as long as the spikelet . . . . .
. . . . STENOTAPHRUM

First glume pitted, as long as the spikelet . . . . . . COELORACHIS

Group II (two to several simple primary branches)

Spikelets with usually three or more bisexual florets

Inflorescence branches paired, whorled, or clustered at the stem tip

Glumes and lemmas awnless; branch axis not stiffly projecting beyond
the terminal spikelet . . . . ELEUSINE

Glumes or lemmas awned; branch axis projecting beyond the terminal
spikelet . . . . DACTYLOCTENIUM

Inflorescence branches scattered along the main stem, seldom more
than one per node

Lowermost branches often with short, spurlike branches at their
bases; spikelets widely spaced on branches . . . .
. . . . ERAGROSTIS (*E. sessilispica*)

Lowermost branches without spurlike branches at their bases; spikelets rather closely spaced on branches . . . . LEPTOCHLOA

Spikelets with a single bisexual floret; reduced florets present or absent

Spikelets with one or two florets above the bisexual one; lemma of bisexual floret with a strong midnerve and two lateral nerves, with
about the same texture as the second glume . . . . Subgroup A

Spikelets with one reduced (neuter or male) floret below the bisexual
one and no reduced florets above; lemma of bisexual floret nerveless, thick and shiny, much firmer than the second glume . . . . . .
. . . . Subgroup AA

Subgroup A (one bisexual floret, no reduced floret below)

Spikelets on the main inflorescence axis as well as on branches . . . .
. . . . SCHEDONNARDUS

Spikelets all on branches, none on the main inflorescence axis, the latter
sometimes terminating in a single branch

Inflorescence branches two or more, clustered or in one to three whorls
at the stem tip

Rudimentary florets absent or represented by a minute scale; inflorescence branches in a single whorl, usually two to six; spikelets awnless . . . . CYNODON

Rudimentary floret or florets present above a perfect (seed-bearing) one; inflorescence branches few to numerous; spikelets usually awned

Glumes linear to lanceolate in side view, the upper one rounded, pointed or minutely awned: lemma of the perfect (seed-bearing) floret usually conspicuously awned; spikelets greenish or dark .... CHLORIS

Glumes lanceolate to oblong in side view, the upper usually short-awned from between rounded lobes; lemma of the perfect (seed-bearing) floret minutely awned; spikelets becoming dark brown at maturity .... EUSTACHYS

Inflorescence branches one to several, scattered on the main axis, not radial, clustered or in whorls

Spikelets one-flowered, without rudimentary florets; inflorescence branches erect and appressed or somewhat spreading, mostly 3–12 cm long .... SPARTINA

Spikelets with one or more rudimentary florets above the perfect (seed-bearing) one; inflorescence branches spreading or bent backwards, infrequently over 4 cm long .... BOUTELOUA

Subgroup AA (one bisexual floret, one reduced floret below)

First glume absent or very short

Lemma of bisexual (upper) floret with a short awn; cuplike or disclike ring present at the base of the spikelet .... ERIOCHLOA

Lemma of bisexual (upper) floret not short-awned; cuplike or disclike ring not present at the base of the spikelet

Lemma of bisexual floret with a rounded back turned away from the central axis; spikelets stalkless or short-stalked, narrowly oblong, pointed at the apex

Spikelets in pairs of one stalkless and one stalked or in unequally stalked pairs................................. DIGITARIA

Spikelets uniformly stalkless or nearly so .... AXONOPUS

Lemma of bisexual floret with a rounded back turned towards the central stem; spikelets stalkless or nearly so, broadly ovate, oblong, or suborbicular

First glume present .... PASPALIDIUM

First glume absent .... PASPALUM

First glume as long as or only slightly shorter than the second glume

Spikelets awnless, not paired or in threes ..... PANICUM (*P. obtusum*)

Spikelets awned, in pairs of one stalkless and one stalked or with one stalkless and two stalked at the branch tips

Inflorescence branches two to six

Upper spikelet stalks and central stem joints with a central

groove .... BOTHRIOCHLOA *(B. ischaemum)*
Upper spikelet stalks and central stem joints flat or rounded ....
.... ANDROPOGON
Inflorescence with eight to numerous branches
Stalked and stalkless spikelets both awned .... ERIANTHUS
Stalked spikelets awnless; stalkless spikelets awned ....
.... BOTHRIOCHLOA

Group III (primary inflorescence branches rebranched; spikelets with one bisexual floret or one male or one female floret)

Spikelets awnless, with glumes large, equal, laterally compressed and keeled, much larger than the firm, pointed, bisexual floret; inflorescence a dense, contracted, cylindrical panicle 3–7 cm long ......
.... PHALARIS
Spikelets awnless or awned, with large or small rounded glumes or glumes absent; inflorescence contracted or open
Spikelets with one reduced (neuter or male) floret below the bisexual one and no reduced florets above
First glume as long as the spikelet; spikelets usually awned, in pairs of one stalkless and one stalked or in threes with one stalkless and two stalked (in *Sorghastrum* the stalked spikelets represented by the stalk only)
Spikelets all alike and bisexual
Stalked spikelets present, like the stalkless ones ... ERIANTHUS
Stalked spikelets completely reduced, represented by the stalk only .... SORGHASTRUM
Spikelets not all alike, the stalked ones male or neuter and smaller in size
Inflorescence an open, much-branched panicle ..... SORGHUM
Inflorescence a contracted panicle with little-branched spikelike primary branches .... BOTHRIOCHLOA
First glume much shorter than the spikelet or absent; if present and nearly as long as the spikelet, then the spikelets not in pairs or threes
Spikelets all or in part subtended by one to several bristles .....
.... SETARIA
Spikelets not subtended by bristles
Tip of the palea of the upper (bisexual) floret usually abruptly pointed; tip of the palea free from the lemma ....
.... ECHINOCHLOA

Key to the Genera of the Grasses : 251

Tip of the palea of the upper (bisexual) floret enclosed by the lemma

Lemma of the upper floret firm but thin and flexible, the margins not inrolled over the margins of the palea; first glume minute or absent

Spikelets on long stalks in an open panicle ... LEPTOLOMA

Spikelets stalkless or on short, appressed stalks of an inflorescence with spikelike primary or secondary branches .... DIGITARIA

Lemma of the upper floret relatively thick and rigid, the margins inrolled over the palea; first glume present

First glume hairless, second glume densely hairy .... BRACHIARIA *(B. ciliatissima)*

First and second glumes both hairless

Plants annual or perennial, flowering in the warm season only, without a basal whorl of short, broad blades

Lemma of upper (bisexual) floret rough; plants annual .... BRACHIARIA

Lemma of upper floret smooth; annuals and perennials .... PANICUM

Plants cool-season perennials, developing a basal whorl of short, broad blades during the winter and early spring........................ DICHANTHELIUM

Spikelets without a reduced floret below the bisexual one; reduced florets absent or one or two reduced or rudimentary florets present above the bisexual one; lemma of bisexual floret with a strong midnerve and often with lateral nerves, usually about the same texture as the second glume when glumes are present

Glumes absent or rudimentary

Spikelets bisexual, strongly compressed laterally; annual; the cultivated rice .... ORYZA

Spikelets unisexual (male or female), not strongly compressed laterally; tall perennial, with male and female spikelets in the same panicle........................... ZIZANIOPSIS

Glumes present

Glumes and lemmas awnless .... Subgroup B

Glumes or lemmas awned .... Subgroup BB

Subgroup B (glumes and lemmas awnless)

Lemma with a tuft of hairs at the base (on the callus); spikelets 7–10 mm long .... CALAMOVILFA

Lemma without a tuft of hairs at the base; spikelets less than 7 mm long

Glumes both as long as or longer than the lemma .... AGROSTIS

Glumes, at least the first, shorter than the lemma ...... SPOROBOLUS

Subgroup BB (glumes or lemmas awned)

Spikelets breaking off below the glumes; glumes equal or nearly so, as
    long as or longer than the lemma
    Glumes awned .... POLYPOGON
    Glumes awnless
        Inflorescence compact, cylindrical; lemma awned from below the
           middle .... ALOPECURUS
        Inflorescence not compact and cylindrical; lemma awned from or near
           the tip...................................... LIMNODIA
Spikelets breaking off above the glumes
    Lemma firm or hard, awned, permanently enclosing the grain; spike-
        lets with a well-developed callus at the base
        Awn of lemma three-branched, the lateral awns short or rudimentary
           in a few species................................ ARISTIDA
        Awn of lemma unbranched............................ STIPA
    Lemma not firm or hard, not permanently enclosing the grain; spike-
        lets with or without a well-developed callus at the base
        Lemma awned from back, base, or cleft tip; glumes equaling or ex-
           ceeding lemma................................. AGROSTIS
        Lemma awned from an undivided or minutely forked tip; glumes,
           at least the first, usually shorter than the lemma ....
           .... MUHLENBERGIA

Group IV (panicle with rebranched primary branches; perfect florets two or more)

Plants 2–6 m tall
    Spikelets mostly 3–7 cm long with seven to thirteen flowers ....
        .... ARUNDINARIA
    Spikelets less than 2 cm long and with fewer than seven flowers
        Leaves mostly basal, the blades 0.5–1.5 cm broad; stems densely
           clumped, without creeping rhizomes .... CORTADERIA
        Leaves evenly distributed on the stem, blades 2–6 cm broad; stems
           with stout, creeping rhizomes, forming large colonies
           Lemmas soft-haired; axis of spikelet (rachilla) hairless ... ARUNDO
           Lemmas hairless; axis of spikelet (rachilla) soft-haired ....
           .... PHRAGMITES
Plants less than 2 m tall
    Lemmas with three nerves, these usually conspicuous ... Subgroup C
    Lemmas, at least some, with five to fifteen nerves, the nerves conspic-
        uous or obscure .... Subgroup CC

Subgroup C (lemmas three-nerved)

Nerves of lemma finely hairy, or the base of the lemma long-haired
    Panicles 1–8 cm long, contracted, ovoid or oblong; lemmas conspic-
        uously long-haired on the nerves, at least below ... ERIONEURON
    Panicles open or contracted, 4–30 cm or more long; when panicle less
        than 10 cm long, then the lemmas inconspicuously minutely
        downy on the nerves .... TRIDENS
Nerves of lemma not downy or minutely downy; base of lemma not long-
    haired
    Lemmas three-awned .... SCLEROPOGON
    Lemmas awnless .... ERAGROSTIS

Subgroup CC (lemmas with five to fifteen nerves)

Lemmas awned .... Subgroup D
Lemmas awnless .... Subgroup DD

Subgroup D (lemmas awned)

Lemmas with nine or more awns or awnlike lobes
    Lemmas with nine subequal, feathery awns .... ENNEAPOGON
    Lemmas with eleven or more hairless awns of irregular lengths .....
        .... PAPPOPHORUM
Lemmas with a single awn
    Stems woody, perennial; spikelets mostly 3–7 cm long ... ARUNDINARIA
    Stems not woody or perennial; spikelets rarely as much as 3 cm long
        Glumes 2 cm or more long; lemmas 1.5 cm or more long; introduced
            annual .... AVENA
        Glumes less than 2 cm long, or if longer, then the lemmas less than
            1.5 cm long
            First glume with three or five distinct nerves; glumes and lemmas
                rounded on the back; lemmas 8–12 mm long, excluding the
                awns
                Plants perennial; palea not adherent to the grain ..... MELICA
                Plants perennial or annual; palea adherent to the grain ......
                .... BROMUS
            First glume with one or three distinct or indistinct nerves; glumes
                and lemmas keeled or rounded on the back
            Palea colorless
                Second glume obovate, broadest above the middle; spikelets
                    breaking off below the glumes .... SPHENOPHOLIS
                Second glume broadest below the middle; spikelets breaking
                    off above the glumes .... KOELERIA
            Palea green or brown, at least on the nerves

Spikelets 1.5 (infrequently 1.2) cm or more long; lemma tip
distinctly to minutely two-pronged . . . . BROMUS
Spikelets less than 1.2 cm long
Lemmas awned from a distinctly two-pronged tip, the awn
straight or bent; second glume equaling or exceeding
the lowermost floret . . . . SPHENOPHOLIS
Lemmas awned from an undivided or minutely notched tip,
the awn straight; second glume usually shorter than
the lowermost floret
Plants annual . . . . VULPIA
Plants perennial . . . . FESTUCA

Subgroup DD (lemmas awnless)

Glumes and lemmas inflated and papery, spreading at right angles to the
spikelet axis (rachilla), resembling the rattles of a rattlesnake; plants
annual . . . . BRIZA
Glumes and lemmas not as above; plants annual or perennial
Lowermost one to three florets reduced, sterile, about half as long as
those above
Spikelets breaking off below the glumes, the spikelets falling entire;
plants of coastal dunes . . . . UNIOLA
Spikelets breaking off above the glumes and between the florets;
plants of woodland sites . . . . CHASMANTHIUM
Lowermost florets not reduced, as large as those above
Palea colorless; lateral nerves of the lemma indistinct
Second glume obovate, usually abruptly narrowing to a broadly
rounded tip; spikelets breaking off below the glumes . . . . . .
. . . . SPHENOPHOLIS
Second glume not broadened above the middle or only slightly so,
pointed at the tip; spikelets breaking off above the glumes . . . .
. . . . KOELERIA
Palea green or brown, at least on the nerves
Lemmas with seven to thirteen nerves
Spikelets unisexual, the male and the female in separate in-
florescences and usually on separate plants; glumes and
lemmas thick, firm, indistinctly nerved . . . . DISTICHLIS
Spikelets with both stamens and pistils; glumes and lemmas
relatively thin, the lemmas mostly with distinct nerves
and membranous margins
Palea sticking to the grain at maturity . . . . BROMUS
Palea not sticking to the grain at maturity . . . . MELICA

Lemmas five-nerved

    Lemmas narrowly or broadly pointed at the tip, not papery on the margins .... FESTUCA

    Lemmas rounded or only slightly jointed at the tip, usually papery on the margins

        Glumes and lemmas spreading at right angles to the spikelet axis (rachilla), inflated and papery, resembling the rattles of a rattlesnake .... BRIZA

        Glumes and lemmas not as above .... POA

Glossary

ACUMINATE. Gradually tapering to a point.

ACUTE. Sharp-pointed, not abruptly or lengthily extended, but making an angle of less than 90°.

ADVENTITIOUS ROOTS. Roots not developed from the primary root system; roots developed from stem, leaf, or flower structures.

ANNUAL. Of one season's or year's duration from seed to maturity and death.

ANTHER. The pollen-bearing part of the stamen.

APEX. The tip of an organ.

APICAL. Situated at or forming the apex.

APPRESSED. Pressed closely against or fitting closely to something.

ARTICULATION. A joint or node.

AURICLE. An ear-shaped appendage; the name is applied to pointed appendages that occur laterally at the base of the leaf blade in some grasses and laterally at the sheath apex in others.

AWN. A bristle or stiff, hairlike projection; in the grass spikelet, usually the prolongation of the midnerve or lateral nerves of the glumes, lemmas, or palea.

AWN COLUMN. In *Aristida* the three awns of the lemma are fused together below to form a short or long cylindrical column. A similar awn column is present in the spikelets of some *Bouteloua* species, in which the upper floret is reduced to a cylindrical rudiment with three awns at the tip.

AXIL. The upper angle formed between two structures such as the main stem and a branch or spikelet stalk.

AXILLARY. In an axil.

AXIS (of inflorescence, spikelet, etc.). The central stem or branch upon which the parts or organs are arranged.

BIFID. Deeply two-pronged.

BILATERAL. Two-sided; arranged on opposite sides.

BISEXUAL. With both male and female flower structures, that is, stamens and pistils.

BLADE. The expanded portion of a flattened structure such as a leaf or flower petal. The blade of the grass leaf is the usually flattened, expanded portion above the sheath.

BRACT. A modified leaf subtending a flower or belonging to an inflorescence; the glumes, lemma, and palea of the grass spikelet are bracts.

BRISTLE. A stiff hair or hairlike projection.

BUR. A rough or prickly covering around seeds, fruits, or spikelets, such as the bur of the grassbur or sandbur, *Cenchrus*.

CALLUS. The hard, usually pointed base of the spikelet (as in *Heteropogon, Andropogon*, and related genera) or of the floret (as in *Aristida* and *Stipa*) just above the point of disarticulation.

CARTILAGINOUS. Firm and tough but flexible; like cartilage.

CARYOPSIS. A dry, hard, one-seeded fruit which remains closed at maturity with the thin ovary wall stuck to the seed coat; the characteristic grass fruit.

CILIATE. Fringed with hairs.

CLEFT. Cut or divided into lobes.

COLLAR. The outer side of a grass leaf at the junction of the blade and the sheath.

CONCAVE. Hollowed out.

CORDATE. Heart-shaped; with a broad, notched base.

CULM. The stem of a grass.

DECIDUOUS. Falling, as the leaves from a tree.

DECUMBENT. Applied to stems that curve upward from a reclining or horizontal base.

DEPAUPERATE. Impoverished, stunted.

DICHOTOMOUS. Dividing or forking into two equal parts; dichotomous branching is repeatedly branching into pairs.

DIFFUSE. Scattered; dispersed; spreading.

DIGITATE. Radiating from a common point or base, as the finger (digits) of the hand; common bermudagrass, *Cynodon dactylon*, has an inflorescence of digitately arranged spikelike branches.

DIOECIOUS. Unisexual, with staminate and pistillate flowers on separate plants.

DISARTICULATE. To separate at the joints or nodes at maturity.

DORSAL. The back side or surface; the surface turned away from the central stalk or axis; the abaxial surface.

ELLIPSOIDAL. An elliptic solid, twice as long as broad and rounded at the ends.

ELLIPTIC. In the form of a flattened circle, more than twice as long as broad.

ENTIRE. Undivided; in reference to leaves or bracts, the margins continuous, without teeth or lobes.

EXSERTED. Projecting beyond the surrounding parts, as a stamen or stigma.

FASCICLE. A cluster or close bunch, usually used in reference to stems, leaves, or branches of the inflorescence.

FILIFORM. Threadlike; filamentous.

FIRST GLUME. Lowermost of the two glumes.

FLORET. As applied to grasses, the lemma and palea with the enclosed flower. The floret may be perfect, pistillate, staminate, or neuter.

GENICULATE. Abruptly bent, as at the elbow or knee joint.

GIBBOUS. Swollen on one side; with a pouchlike swelling.

GLABRATE. Becoming glabrous; somewhat glabrous.

GLABROUS. Without hairs.

GLAND, GLANDULAR TISSUE. Most "glands" or glandular areas of grass structures are small, circular, elevated or depressed areas of specialized tissue or simply discolored or swollen bands or blotches of discolored tissue. These "glands" sometimes secrete oils or other substances.

GLAUCOUS. Covered or whitened with a waxy bloom, as a cabbage leaf or a plum.

GLOBOSE. Spherical or rounded; globelike.

GLUMES. The pair of bracts usually present at the base of the spikelet below the floret or florets.

GRAIN. In respect to grasses, the unhusked or threshed fruit; used in reference to the mature ovary alone or the ovary enclosed in persistent bracts (palea, lemma, glumes).

HERBAGE. The stems and leaves of a plant.

HIRSUTE. Provided with coarse and stiff hairs, these long, straight, and erect or ascending.

HISPID. Provided with erect, rigid, bristly hairs.

HYALINE. Transparent or translucent.

IMBRICATE. Overlapping, as the shingles of a roof.

IMPERFECT. Unisexual flowers or florets; with either male or female reproductive structures but not both.

INFLORESCENCE. The flowering portion of a shoot; in grasses, the spikelets and the axis or branch system that supports them, the inflorescence being delimited at the base by the uppermost leafy node of the shoot.

INTERNODE. The portion of the stem or other structure between two nodes.

INVOLUCRE. A circle or cluster of bracts or reduced branchlets that surround a flower or floret or a group of flowers or florets.

INVOLUTE. Rolled inward from the edges.

JOINT. A stem, spikelet, or inflorescence axis internode together with a portion of the node at either end; generally used in reference to the units of a disarticulating stem, spikelet axis, or inflorescence axis.

KEEL. A prominent dorsal ridge like the keel of a boat. Glumes and lemmas of laterally compressed spikelets are often sharply keeled; the palea of some florets is two-keeled.

LANCEOLATE. Lance-shaped; relatively narrow, tapering to both ends from a point below the middle.

LEMMA. The lowermost of the two bracts enclosing the flower in the grass floret.

LIGULE. A membranous or hairy appendage on the adaxial surface of the grass leaf at the junction of sheath and blade.

LINEAR. Long and narrow and with parallel margins.

MEMBRANOUS. Thin, soft, and pliable, with the character of a membrane.

MONOECIOUS. Flowers unisexual, with male and female flowers borne on the same plant.

MUCRO. A short, small, abrupt tip of an organ, as the projection of a nerve of the leaf.

MUCRONATE. With a mucro.

NERVE. A simple vein or slender rib of a leaf or bract.

NEUTER. Without functional stamens or pistils.

NODE. Region of stem, branch, or spikelet axis at which leaves, bracts, or branches are produced.

OBLONG. Two to three times longer than broad and with nearly parallel sides.

OBOVATE. Inversely egg-shaped (as in longitudinal section), with the broader end near the apex.

OBTUSE. Blunt or rounded, making an angle of 90° or more.

ORBICULAR. Spherical.

OVARY. The enlarged lower part of the pistil which encloses the ovules or young seeds.

OVATE. Egg-shaped (in longitudinal section), with the broadest end toward the base.

PALEA. The uppermost of the two bracts enclosing the grass flower in the floret; the palea usually is two-nerved and two-keeled.

PANICLE. As applied to grasses, any inflorescence in which the spikelets are not stalkless or individually stalked on the main axis.

PAPILLA (pl. PAPILLAE). A minute, nipple-shaped projection.

PAPILLA-BASED HAIRS. Hairs arising from papillae; hairs with thick, swollen bases.

PEDICEL. The stalk of a single flower; in grasses, the stalk of a single spikelet.

PEDUNCLE. The stalk of a flower cluster; in grasses, the stalk of a spikelet cluster.

PERENNIAL. Living for more than one year.

PERFECT. A flower or floret with both male and female functional reproductive structures.

PERSISTENT. Persisting; in reference to the inflorescence or spikelet axis, one that does not disarticulate.

PETIOLE. A leaf stalk.

PILOSE. With soft, straight hairs.

PISTIL. The female (seed-bearing) structures of the flower, ordinarily consisting of the ovary and one or more styles and stigmas.

PISTILLATE. Having a pistil but not stamens.

PRIMARY INFLORESCENCE BRANCH. Branch arising directly from the main inflorescence axis.

PUBERULENT. Minutely pubescent.

PUBESCENT. Downy or soft-haired.

RACEME. As applied to grasses, an inflorescence in which all the spikelets are borne on stalks inserted directly on the main (undivided) inflorescence axis or in which some spikelets are stalkless and some stalked on the main axis.

RACHILLA. The axis of a grass spikelet.

RACHILLA JOINT. See JOINT.

RACHIS. The axis of a spike, raceme, or spikelike inflorescence branch.

REDUCED FLORET. A staminate or neuter floret; if highly reduced, then termed a rudimentary floret.

REFLEXED. Bent or angled backwards at more than a 90° angle from the axis or surface of the plant structure.

RETRORSE. Pointed downward or toward the base.

RHIZOME. An underground stem, usually with scale leaves and adventitious roots borne at regularly spaced nodes.

ROSETTE. A whorl or cluster of basal leaves.

RUDIMENT. In the grass spikelet, one or more rudimentary florets.

SCABROUS. Rough to the touch, usually because of the presence of minute prickle-hairs (spicules) in the epidermis.

SECOND GLUME. The uppermost of the two glumes of a spikelet.

SERRATE. Saw-toothed, with sharp teeth pointing forward.

SESSILE. Inserted directly, without a stalk.

SETACEOUS. Bristly or bristlelike.

SHEATH (OF LEAF). In grasses and sedges, the basal portion of the leaf, the part that encloses the stem.

SPATHE. A large bract enclosing an inflorescence.

SPICATE. Spikelike.

SPICULE. Short, stout, pointed projection of the leaf epidermis; spicules often grade into prickle-hairs.

SPIKE. An inflorescence with flowers or spikelets stalkless on an elongated, unbranched main axis.

SPIKELET. The basic unit of the grass inflorescence, usually consisting of a short axis, the rachilla, bearing two "empty" bracts, the glumes, at the basal nodes and one or more florets above. Each floret consists usually of two bracts, the lemma (lower) and the palea (upper), and a flower. The flower usually includes two lodicules, three stamens, and a pistil.

STAMEN. The male organ of the flower, consisting of a pollen-bearing anther on a filament.

STAMINATE. Having stamens but not pistils.

STIGMA. The part of the ovary or style that receives the pollen for effective fertilization.

STOLON. A modified horizontal stem that loops or runs along the surface of the ground and serves to spread the plant by rooting at the nodes.

STOLONIFEROUS. With stolons.

STYLE. The contracted portion of the pistil between the ovary and the stigma.

SUBTEND. To be below and close to.

SUCCULENT. Fleshy or juicy.

TERMINAL. Growing at the end of a branch or stem, as a bud, inflorescence, or the like.

THROAT. The adaxial portion of the grass leaf at the junction of sheath and blade.

TRANSVERSE. Lying or being across or in a cross direction.

TRIFURACATE. Having three forks or branches.

TRUNCATE. Terminating abruptly as if cut off transversely; appearing "chopped off."

TURGID. Swollen, tightly drawn by pressure from within.

UNDULANT, UNDULATING. Gently wavy.

UNILATERAL. One-sided; developed or hanging on one side.

UNISEXUAL. With either male or female sex structures but not both.

VESTIGIAL. Rudimentary and almost completely reduced, with only a vestige remaining.

VILLOUS. Bearing long, soft, unmatted hairs.
VISCID. Sticky; glutinous.

WHORL. A ring of similar parts radiating from a node.

Index

(page numbers of illustrations in bold face)

Guide to the Current Names of the Grasses
BY STEPHAN L. HATCH

Page	Old Name	Current Name
x	*Aristida roemeriana*	*Aristida purpurea* var. *purpurea*
x	*Aristida wrightii*	*Aristida purpurea* var. *wrightii*
5, 10	*Agropyron smithii*	*Elytrigia smithii*
5, 6	Bermudagrass	bermudagrass
6	Johnsongrass	johnson grass
11	*Agropyron smithii* Rydb.	*Elytrigia smithii* (Rydb.) Nevski
12	*Agrostis hiemalis*	*Agrostis hyemalis*
13	*Agrostis hiemalis* (Walt.) B.S.P.	*Agrostis hyemalis* (Walt.) B.S.P.
21	Roemer threeawn, *A. roemeriana*	Purple threeawn, *A. purpurea* var. *purpurea*
22	*A. longiseta*	*A. purpurea* var. *longiseta*
22	*A. purpurea*	*A. purpurea* var. *purpurea*
22	*A. wrightii*	*A. purpurea* var. *wrightii*
24	*Aristida longiseta* Steud.	*Aristida purpurea* Nutt. var. *longiseta* (Steud.) Vasey
25	*Aristida longiseta*	*Aristida purpurea* var. *longiseta*
29	Roemer threeawn, *Aristida roemeriana*	Purple threeawn, *Aristida purpurea* Nutt. *var. purpurea*
30	*Aristida wrightii*	*Aristida purpurea* var. *wrightii*
31	*Aristida wrightii*	*Aristida purpurea* Nutt. var. *wrightii* (Nash) Allred
38	*B. saccharoides* var. *torreyana*	*B. laguroides* ssp. *torreyana*
38	*B. saccharoides* var. *longipaniculata*	*B. longipaniculata*

Page	Old Name	Current Name
41	*Bothriochloa ischaemum* (L.) var. *songarica* (Rupr.) Celerier & Harlan	*Bothriochloa ischaemum* (L.) Keng var. *songarica* Keng. (Fisch & Mey.) Celerier & Harlan
41	*Bothriochloa saccharoides* (Swartz) Rydb.	*Bothriochloa laguroides* (DC.) Herter
42	*Bothriochloa saccharoides* var. torreyana	*Bothriochloa laguroides* ssp. *torreyana*
42	*Bothriochloa saccharoides* var. *longipaniculata* (Gould) Gould	*Bothriochloa longipaniculata* (Gould) Allred & Gould
42	*Bothriochloa sacchariodes* var. *torreyana* (Steud.) Gould	*Bothriochloa laguroides* (DC.) Herter ssp. *torreyana* (Steud.) Allred & Gould
43	*Bothriochloa saccharoides* var. *longipaniculata*	*Bothriochloa longipaniculata* (Gould) Allred & Gould
44	*Bothriochloa saccharoides* var. *torreyana*	*Bothriochloa laguroides* ssp. *torreyana*
74	*C. ciliaris*	*Pennisetum ciliare*
74	*Cenchrus ciliaris* L.	*Pennisetum ciliare* (L.) Link
75	*Cenchrus ciliaris*	*Pennisetum ciliare*
78, 79	Longleaf chasmanthium	Longleaf woodoats
87	*Dactyloctenium aegyptium* (L.) Willd.	*Dactyloctenium aegyptium* (L.) Beauv.
89	Roundseed dichanthelium	Roundseed rosettegrass
89	Openflower dichanthelium	Openflower rosettegrass
89, 90	Woolly dichanthelium	Woolly rosettegrass
91, 92	Openflower dichanthelium	Openflower rosettegrass
93, 94	Scribner dichanthelium	Scribner rosettegrass
94, 95	Roundseed dichanthelium	Roundseed rosettegrass
96	Southern crabgrass, *D. ciliaris*	Hairy crabgrass, *D. sanguinalis*
99	Southern crabgrass, *D. ciliaris* (Retz.) Koel.	Hairy crabgrass, *Digitaria sanguinalis* (L.) Scop.
100	Southern crabgrass, *Digitaria ciliaris*	Hairy crabgrass, *Digitaria sanguinalis*
103	*E. colona*	*E. colonum*

Page	Old Name	Current Name
103, 104	*Echinochloa colona*	*Echinochloa colonum*
115	*Eragrostis cilianensis* (All.) E. Mosher	*Eragrostis cilianensis* (All.) Janchen
145	*Leptoloma*	*Digitaria*
145	*Leptoloma cognatum* (Schult.) Chase	*Digitaria cognata* (Schult.) Pilger
146	*Leptoloma cognatum*	*Digitaria cognata*
210, 211	Yellow Indiangrass	Yellow indiangrass
248	*Agropyron*	*Elytrigia*
252	*Leptoloma*	*Digitaria*
265	Bermudagrass	bermudagrass
265	chasmanthium	woodoats
265	Gulf	gulf
265	Dallisgrass	dallisgrass
265	dichanthelium	rosettegrass
266	Indiangrass	indiangrass
266	Johnsongrass	johnsongrass
266	Junegrass	junegrass
266	Kleingrass	kleingrass
266	Ozarkgrass	ozarkgrass
266	Rhodesgrass	rhodesgrass
267	Vaseygrass	vaseygrass